AGENDA
FOR
INVENTION

Arthur W. Foshay
Professor of Education
Teachers College
Columbia University

SCHOOLS
FOR THE 70'S

Published by the National Education Association
Center for the Study of Instruction (CSI)

PRELIMINARY SERIES

Single copy: paperbound, $1.50 (Stock No. 381-11946); cloth-bound, $3.00 (Stock No. 381-11948). Discounts on quantity orders: 2-9 copies, 10 percent; 10 or more copies, 20 percent. All orders must be prepaid except for those on official purchase order forms. Shipping and handling charges will be added to billed orders. Order from Publications-Sales Section, National Education Association, 1201 Sixteenth Street, N.W., Washington, D.C. 20036.

CONTENTS

ACKNOWLEDGMENTS

Many people have been helpful to me in the preparation of this book. I, of course, take full responsibility for what it says. I especially want to acknowledge the thoughtful help of Lois Karasik of NEA's Center for the Study of Instruction. Among others I wish specifically to acknowledge Dr. Ole Sand, director of CSI, and also Dr. Robert McClure and Fred Husmann, both of CSI; Dr. Dorothy Fraser of Hunter College; Dr. Sidney Marland, head of the Institute for Educational Development; Dr. Bruce Joyce; and Dr. Richard Burkhardt.

Arthur W. Foshay
Professor of Education
Teachers College
Columbia University
September 1970

FOREWORD

"One of the consistent demands of the future," says the author of this volume, "is that the schools be directly resonant with the world as it really is." Such a view is a welcome change from what teachers have come to expect from a book about curriculum. Foshay's freshly delineated look at our nation's schools as they have evolved and, more importantly, his inventive proposals for change illustrate a perspective that is immediate, realistic, and sensitive to the world of the teacher.

As part of the Preliminary Series of NEA's SCHOOLS FOR THE 70's program, *Curriculum for the 70's: An Agenda for Invention* is directed to the United Profession as it continues the welcome but awesome task of promoting ideal schools. Carefully conceived and thoughtfully developed, Foshay's suggestions for a revitalized curriculum can serve as the focus for increased effort toward a curriculum that is meaningful and, at the same time, responsive to the needs, interests, and abilities of learners. Central to this break from traditional curriculum is the belief that the key to successful and lasting change is increased decision making by teachers.

Moving beyond the usual plea for a more humane schooling experience, Foshay delineates what the components of that experience might be. Further, he provides in-practice as well as hypothetical examples of what actual school programs might look like, how learners might behave, what consequences might result, and what the changed role of the teacher might be. In short, the volume is a unique combination of a soundly formulated rationale for developing a curriculum and an equally sound guide to practice.

In addition to the Preliminary Series, of which this book is a part, the NEA's SCHOOLS FOR THE 70's program will include a

1

comprehensive, single-volume report, with accompanying multi-media and action programs addressed to all members of the profession and the public. Already in circulation is an Auxiliary Series of four volumes addressed primarily to curriculum specialists and university and school researchers. This major publication and action program of the NEA's Center for the Study of Instruction (CSI) is evidence of the NEA's deeply-held commitment to the improvement of instruction and to the central role of the teacher in any design for change.

Helen Bain
President
National Education Association
September 1970

Chapter 1. The Setting and the Problems

Institutions are the prisoners of their central purposes. If the central purpose changes, then the institution must change to match it. It is the basic assumption of this commentary that the central purpose of education as we know it has changed, that a new conception of purpose is necessary, and that therefore some fundamental changes in the practices and forms of education are required.

The central function of education until now has been to serve the needs of society. This is a noble purpose. It was Jefferson's, when he declared that the schools were necessary to prepare the people for citizenship. As a purpose, it infused with meaning the curriculum of the 19th century and most of the 20th. But in our time, it looks insufficient. The schools as servants of society seek to meet society's needs: for an informed, critical citizenry, able to function economically and socially, able to participate in the democratic institutions that are the fabric of the country.

Now, however, an additional demand is being made on education—the same demand that is made on the mature by the young: that education contribute to self-fulfillment. But self-fulfillment was never a *social* imperative. When the needs for self-fulfillment and the needs of society have come into conflict, the schools have resolved in favor of social needs—for, after all, the meeting of social needs has been the central purpose of the schools. Such a resolution has had dreadful consequences. The single-minded pursuit of social needs has led the schools to practice a social-class bias that has excluded millions of students from education at an early age. It has led the schools to reinforce the subtle racism that permeates the institution. When the schools do no more than reflect society's needs, they become enormous screening devices, by means of which those most needed by society are located early and given special treatment. The schools, one may say, are organized around the presumption of ultimate failure. If a child isn't held back early in his career (and about 20 percent of all American children repeat a grade during the first three years of schooling), he is nevertheless ultimately defeated by the system. He fails to finish high school, or to gain entrance to college, or to "make" graduate school, or to win a doctorate, or to publish his dissertation to general acclaim. Sooner or later, he loses. Eventually, the system excludes almost everyone. It is not so much that the schools foster the pursuit of excellence. Rather, they pursue the excellent. The others are rejected.

It won't do. Instead of acting as if what is good for the country is good for the individual, we have to go back to the principles of the Founding Fathers: what is good for the individual is good for the country. The function of the educational enterprise is not only to meet social needs. It has to meet the need of the individual for self-fulfillment as well.

We teachers have to learn what this change in our central purpose means. To do so, we have to learn to look beyond our immediate work and to assess the meanings that crowd in on us from the world we live in. We shall try to do that here, in this first section. We shall do it with some diffidence, because we are not expert in the analysis of the great questions of our times. We shall do it with much selectivity. While everything that happens has educational implications, not everything is equally pertinent to education. We shall look at what seems most pertinent.

In this first section, we shall begin by looking out on the world from a teacher's viewpoint. Having done that, we shall look at teaching as it appears now, for it has changed during the past 10 years. We shall try to discern the possibilities and limitations we have built into our baroque institution. On the basis of these observations and speculations, the kinds of decisions needed during the immediate future should appear, as well as the likely collisions. If our vision has been clear enough, perhaps we shall see the outlines of a resolution of the problems we are caught up in.

It's worth reiterating: if our central purpose has been inadequate, then it must change. But if it changes, everything else will change with it. We shall consider that possibility here. It will take nerve, and it won't be easy. But if our conception of purpose doesn't match what we are doing, we are making an enormous, nationwide mistake, and we have to correct it.

4

THE WORLD FROM THE TEACHER'S POINT OF VIEW

Change in American Society

American education ought to be changing because American society is changing. Not only are our students the product of our society, our educational imperatives are also the product of society. Even if the school *ought to be* a moral enterprise before it is anything else, it surely *is* a social institution before it is anything else. As a social institution, it ought to be relevant to the society it serves.

The external society within which we live—that is, the society of the United States primarily—isn't at all what it was when the schools took their present form. For one thing, it is more and more difficult to talk about an American society without recognizing that it is a part of a larger world society. We are more responsive to our international relationships now than we ever were. We have managed to back ourselves into a most unpopular war. Unlike in earlier times when Thoreau and a few others led the opposition to another war, in our time the intellectual opposition has managed to take advantage of the mass media in such a way as to involve us all in a frightful internal division. We don't have a common enemy in Vietnam, so we turn on one another.

We live in a world without margins, as McLuhan has pointed out. The boundaries of our nation have become indefinite. Our theater, our graphic arts, and our music no longer have definable margins or even definable composition. They seem to emerge from their surroundings as centers of emphases, rather than as discrete spaces. We live on a flow of information so enormous and disjointed as to be almost beyond belief and certainly beyond comprehension in traditional ways. In every way one can think of, we're living as if the process were the meaning, as if the means were the end. We are more in contact with one another, but with less cohesiveness, than we have ever been.

We Americans live in a time of systemwide phenomena. Our internal economic structures are based on the assumption of large-scale foreign trade. Our internal political decisions are overwhelmed by external problems. It's a time of syndromes, such as environmental pollution. It is not a time of individual enterprise in the old sense. We are more interdependent, yet less cohesive.

5

We have come through a period since 1950 of mass internal migrations to the cities. This is by no means a uniquely American phenomenon. It has happened in every large city in the world. They all have housing shortages for the less than rich. Traffic problems that were once more or less amusing have become disastrous. In the United States, only 6 percent of the population now lives on farms, and the percentage will drop even further. We are an urban civilization. "Today well over 80% of Americans live in towns and cities with populations over 2,500, and 60% live in some 200 metropolitan areas each having a population of more than 50,000." [1]

Yet even with this migration, American central cities are not so densely populated as they were a half-century ago. Indeed, while the population of most central cities is growing slowly, or not at all, that of the suburbs is exploding.[2] The margin of the city has become indefinite.

"More than half the nation's employed population is not involved in the production of goods but in the provision of services. In occupational terms this has meant a shift from blue to white collar work. The Bureau of Labor Statistics for the period 1960-1975 projects a rate of growth in white collar employment which is twice as great as that for blue collar jobs." [3] The margin between management and labor has become indefinite.

Even the government of the city has become marginless. Governmental leadership is not in the hands of the mayor, but in the case of New York City "other leadership institutions participate indispensably in governing the city—for example, the organized bureaucracies, the many non-governmental groups, the communications media, and the political parties." [4]

With the enormously increased urbanization of our society, coupled with the loss of margins, of framework, has come a new need for identity. The various segments of our population have become more self-conscious in recent years than ever before. The labor unions began the process, giving themselves new identities in the form of occupational categories. Now, however, all sorts of

---

[1] Connery, Robert H., and Caraley, Demetrios. *Governing the City: Challenges and Options for New York.* Proceedings of the Academy of Political Science, Vol. 29, No. 4. New York: Columbia University Press, 1969. p. 3.

[2] *Ibid.*

[3] Tobier, Emanuel. "People and Jobs." *Governing the City, op. cit.* p. 8.

[4] Sayre, Wallace S. "City Hall Leadership." *Governing the City, op. cit.* p. 39.

groups have become aware of themselves as groups and are active politically, economically, and culturally. The melting pot has long since disappeared as an ideal and with it our sentimental appellations: "Italian-Americans," "Polish-Americans," even "Negro-Americans." Our attempts to see ourselves as an undifferentiated whole have languished until they have now disappeared. The function of the school as the unifying agency, the homogenizing, acculturating agency, has become meaningless in a time when people seek their identity through affiliation with groups, not affiliation with the nation. We are self-consciously members of our various religious groups, our residential areas, our occupational groups, even our avocational groups. These groups, which of course have always existed, have taken on an importance during our period of rapid urbanization that they never had before. They have become a primary means to identity, rather than a useful attribute for certain aspects of living. We are more divided from one another than we were 50 years ago, and our divisions have greater meaning.

The disappearance of the primary group from middle-class life is a little-noted change in our time. There was a time when it was characteristic of middle-class behavior that information about the nation and the world was talked over and interpreted with one's neighbors and friends. The source of information in those days was print. There was a certain distance between the reader and the information, and there was time to interpret. Consequently, neither action nor reaction was as rapid as it is now. Now, we live in an increasingly fictive world, held together by mass communications. The middle-class man lives in several communities simultaneously: his occupation, his peers in other places, his family, his avocational group, and so on. He does not live primarily in his neighborhood. The automobile, the telephone, the mail, the jet plane, and broadcasting have changed all that.

The primary group of neighbors and friends has virtually disappeared from middle-class life. It survives as a principal source of interpretation only in the working class. The middle class has long since left the neighborhood tavern and is rapidly withdrawing from the church and the synagogue, where (as is increasingly and anxiously recognized by some of the clergy) what is talked over is less and less relevant to public life and public affairs.

The effect of this change is to produce yet another split among the many that exist in our society—a split in basic stance between the members of the middle class and the members of the working class. Indeed, if the projections cited above are correct, the working class is on the point of disappearing as a distinct group.

Another change is concerned with the increased impersonality that accompanies increase in population. There is much discussion of the contamination of our environment, especially with the appearance of smog in the largest cities, here and abroad. We face the real possibility of a gross contamination from yet another source—the increase in population in itself. The idea that people are a contaminant has not yet gained a foothold. Yet it must be allowed as a possibility.

What accompanies the enormous worldwide increase in population is an increased impersonality in our dealings with one another. The denser the population, the greater the individual's need for privacy and the more formal and ritualized his relationships with other human beings become. The more prosperous among the inhabitants of the older cities in the world all surround themselves with walls, whether the walls be literally high or more or less impregnable or only symbolic, like fences and hedges. We may expect this tendency to increase in the United States as our population increases. Compared to people of other Western nations, Americans are breezy and informal with one another. We may expect this charming characteristic to wither away during the years ahead. Because there are more of us, we will not know one another so well. The bonds of mutual trust that characterized small-town America of two generations and more ago have already largely disappeared. We may expect them to be replaced with increasingly formal and distrustful arrangements among us.

Yet we are more closely bound together than we ever were. We're bound by the large operational systems within which we live—the industrial systems, the governmental systems, the systems of transportation and communication, the energy systems, the systems of food distribution. We are busy inventing a large-scale system for health. We teachers know very well how elaborate and far flung the educational system is. We move through these systems with great ease. We Americans change dwelling places casually. Unlike other Western countries, we even change our employment casually. It is common for a man to have as many as 10 employers during his working career, not because he is drifting from job to job but because he is building a career. The old notion of the faithful, trusted employee is rapidly disappearing.

The combination of increased mobility, increased interdependence, and increased impersonality produces a demand that we have not yet recognized. The demand is that we have reliable means for recognizing one another quickly. Employers need to have reliable certification in order to know what it means when a man says that he is an accountant, a lawyer, a computer programer, a TV repairman. This need for certification goes all the way through our society. The number of certificates of competency, warranted or possible, can be expected to increase. The demand on the schools to produce such warrantable documents of specific competency may also be expected to increase.

America and the Rest of the World

Teachers, as a group, comprise one of the last segments of our population to become accustomed to the idea that the United States has a dominant position in the world. Nothing has happened to us as a profession that alters the combination of chauvinism and sentimentality that has characterized our view of America's foreign relations. The ideology of the melting pot may have disappeared from public life, but it has not disappeared from our classrooms. We continue, at bottom, to believe that people are more alike than they are different and that it is their alikeness that ought to be at the center of our attention as educators. The notion of cultural pluralism within our own borders has been too difficult for us to grasp. Cultural pluralism as an avenue to understanding that other nations have the same right we have to be what they are and that our relations with them should enhance their integrity, instead of helping them along the road we have traveled, has continued to elude us. We are shocked at the hostility shown to our country—shocked in the same sense that white liberals are shocked at the hostility of black militants, and for most of the same reasons. We have as yet shown next to no ability to look at the United States through the eyes of anyone outside our borders. But there are forces at work that will compel us to do so, and soon.

One of these is that collection of forces we have come to think of as interdependence. We are accustomed to the idea of economic interdependence, though we rarely grasp its immediate implications. We continue to think of ourselves as basically self-sufficient when the facts are contrary. Not only are we dependent on others

obscure and secret social dynamics. It should not be surprising that the phenomenon of school loyalty can become grotesque in these circumstances, that the official school mores have become more and more elemental and rudimentary in character, that what students have in common tends to be not their affiliation with the school but their affiliation with one another.

At the same time, the actual number of students each teacher sees is tending to decrease. Since 1950, the student-teacher ratio has gradually dropped, though not very greatly. During the years ahead, it is likely to drop even more if present trends continue.

There are two reasons for the decline in the student-teacher ratio. One, accurately forecast by the Bureau of the Census in 1950, is that the birth rate has begun to drop sharply. The actual number of students in school can be expected to reflect this drop for a few years, whereupon the new young families being raised by the war babies of the 40's will result in an increase in school population. We are just now entering the second wave of the population fluctuations produced by World War II. We are coming into a period when, if the number of teachers is held constant, the teacher-pupil ratio will drop. A second reason for the lowered pupil-teacher ratio is that 20 years of pressure on the part of the organized profession for increased teacher salaries and more realistic teaching assignments is beginning to pay off.

So the first thing the teacher sees when he looks at students is a larger aggregation of children than existed 20 years ago and opportunities for face-to-face contacts with fewer of them.

But let's look at the students a little more closely, not as numbers but as people. A profound change has taken place among the young people. Despite gross inequalities of opportunity, most of the population has known 40 years of improved and more available education, economic improvement (at least since the beginning of World War II), improved nutrition, and the disappearance of many childhood diseases. The contemporary student is bigger and healthier, matures earlier, and is intellectually more competent than our school customs and even the literature of child development suggest to us. The more articulate among the young, responding both to the new child-society and to their own feelings of competence, are beginning a rebellion against the prolonged infancy that our schools and our employment patterns thrust upon them.

Indeed, the change in the character of young people—at least of those among them who raise the questions and the issues—is everywhere apparent. They seem uninterested in trying to evolve a better life style out of the one that exists. They act alienated at the most profound level. They are ahistorical—the year 1 seems to come up every three years (as this is written, the year 1 appears to have begun with the Democratic National Convention of 1968). Kenneth Rexroth saw it coming as long ago as 1957 when, in an essay called "The Art of the Beat Generation," he described their attitude as *disaffiliation* and correctly foreshadowed the astonishment of the older generation. Most of us, the elders, grew up used to the idea of youthful rebellion. Indeed we saw it as a desirable phase in maturation, during which one became acquainted with society by testing its limits. We ourselves had participated in such a rebellion, and we thought it was healthy. Here, Rexroth pointed out, was a generation that rejected our rebellion! They simply dropped out. They disaffiliated. They acted as if they had lost interest in whatever opinions or wisdom we had about their plight or the nature of things. They created their own rebellion. It was, and is, sufficient from their point of view to respond to our opinions with "you don't dig."

It's a split world, from their point of view and often from ours, as we have already mentioned. It is possible that the schools, having changed very little in spirit for two generations, exacerbate the splits. Here, thanks to Edward J. Meade, Jr.,[5] is a list of such splittings:

> young—old
> black—white
> affluence—poverty
> permissiveness—rigidity
> passiveness—violence
> morality—dogma
> prolonged infancy—earlier maturity
> institutions—anti-institutions
> domestic—foreign
> public—private
> collective security—individualism
> change—order
> hypocrisy—honesty

---

[5] Meade, Edward J., Jr. Remarks at a Seminar on Schools for the 70s, New York, June 1969.

13

. . . to which we might add a few that the schools specifically tend to produce:

> bright—dull
> college—noncollege
> teachers—students
> subject matter—relevance

Let's listen to the terms of the indictment, as summarized by Robert Paul Wolff.

> *First,* modern industrial society in general and American society in particular, is ugly, repressive, destructive and subversive of much that is truly human; *second,* the youthful outbursts of rebellion and dissent are amalgamating into a coherent, though as yet uncompleted, "counter-culture"; *third,* the root of our troubles is Western society's unquestioning acceptance of the "ideology of objective consciousness," the ideal and method of science; and *fourth,* the anti-rationalist counter-culture "that our alienated young are giving shape to . . . looks like the saving vision our endangered civilization requires." [6]

Of these, the most disturbing to the elders is the third. Our whole school system, and indeed our whole governmental structure, is based on the idea that people are rational and that the uses of reason are the main substance of our educational system. What is one to do if, in the face of the injunction, "Let's be reasonable," the response is "No, let's feel right about it"?

The Subject Matter Revolution

Beginning in the mid 50's, a basic change has become apparent in our conception of subject matter. Between 1910 and 1955, the subject matter of the schools was by and large thought of as being somehow derivable from an analysis of child development and of social imperatives. The most interesting experiments in that period were those that sought to relate the offering in subjects to social utility and to child development. Both research and opinion during those years were concerned with these matters. What we now call social relevance was the rule according to which subject matter was to be selected.

After 1955, a profound change in our conception of how subject matter should be selected and developed took place. It began,

---

[6] Wolff, Robert Paul. Review of *The Making of a Counter-Culture* by Theodore Roszak. *New York Times Book Review,* September 7, 1969.

as has been widely noticed, with the scientists and mathematicians, who pointed out that the subject matter as developed at that time had become unhooked from these disciplines as they had been developed by the scholars. Each of these disciplines, it was pointed out, represents a special way of knowing about the world. Each has its own logic of inquiry. Each has its own integrity. To destroy its integrity and to ignore its logic is to risk making the subject matter trivial. Accordingly, through the curriculum projects supported by the National Science Foundation and later by others, a number of these scholars undertook to demonstrate that the basic logic of a field offered strong implications for the way the field might itself be learned. Students were to learn to think like physicists, like chemists, like historians, like geographers, and more recently like literary critics.

Nothing on the same scale had ever happened before in the teaching of the academic subjects. School subject matter before 1910 was a product of its own tradition. A school subject was somebody's contrived pattern of learning activities which, if followed out, would produce a kind of orientation to the subject matter in question. The idea that the student needed more than an orientation was new in 1955. The idea that the logic of inquiry that characterizes any field offers a way of learning that field was new, and it had a vitalizing effect on the subject matter offering.

We are still living with the consequences of this profound change. Its possibilities and intrinsic limitations have become apparent during the years since 1955. Chief among the possibilities is the increase in the significance of the conceptual stuff itself offered in the curriculum (a "key concept" is, after all, a concept of considerable power). For the first time, students were invited to attach themselves to the intellectual mainstream from the very beginning of their schooling. In earlier times, serious intellectuality was postponed until college or later, which meant that for most students the connection was never made. One consequence, therefore, of the subject matter revolution was the development in the lower schools of very large numbers of what might be called junior-grade intellectuals. As they have entered the colleges, the higher education institutions have had to revise upwards the demands and the sophistication of their offerings in one field after another. By 1960, Lee DuBridge, then president of California Institute of Technology, pointed out that the highly selected students entering that institution were no longer content to take the freshman offerings, since they had already mastered such material.

The whole institution, by then, had had to shift itself one step higher to accommodate its students and to meet their impatient demands.

The limitations of the subject matter revolution were not obvious at the beginning to those who developed the new subjects, and they are not obvious even now to many of them. The limitations derived primarily from the fact that the subject matter revisionists concentrated on subject matter at the expense of studying either its relevance to society or its relevance and availability to the children who actually attended schools. The number of students enrolled in high school physics dropped after 1958 from 28 percent of the age group to 18 percent. The accusation that the function of the subject matter revolution was to make better college students, and that alone, was never really countered. Only one obvious implication of the subject matter change has been followed out: the implication that teachers need to be retrained and their preservice education revised in order to make such an offering possible. Accordingly, extensive retraining and revisions have taken place. The new subject matter, when well handled by an experienced, well-educated teacher, is vital and exciting to large proportions of the students who study it, but its own relevance to society is not explicit. The old criterion of "utilization" remains not only unsatisfied but undiscussed. The linkage between the new subjects and child development needs thoughtful consideration.

One further limitation of the subject matter revolution as it has unfolded is its failure to deal with the integration of knowledge within a single human being. The question of how the curriculum is to be designed so that it is reasonable as a whole for a given person remains to be examined. As things stand, the various academic subjects compete with one another for the student's time and attention. Whatever relevance they have for one another is left for the student to detect. The old question of integration of subject matter, dealt with by those who designed the core curriculum two or three generations ago, remains unexamined in these times.

From the teacher's point of view, the subject matter revolution can easily appear as a mere swing of a pendulum—in this case from subject matter (in the teens) to a social base for subject matter (in the 20's, 30's, and 40's) back to subject matter. The fact that the new conception of subject matter bears little relationship to the old is lost in this kind of metaphor. Much more important, however, is that the metaphor itself has always been cynical: nothing really changes, it seems to say. But there is a real change in the conception of academic subject matter. The new concept of curriculum is not a pendulum swing back to what once was. It's not a panacea, either. It appears to be a real improvement, but incomplete.

The old questions won't go away. Without losing any of the new vitality in subject matter, the teacher's task is to cause the subjects to fit one another and the students, at the same time causing them to meet the criterion of social relevance. This is the very least that is required. Given the indictment by the students, described earlier, we have other criteria that must also be met.

The School as an Institution

The organization of the school has increasingly got in the way of certain kinds of changes that many leaders wish to bring about. It does no good to talk about individualizing the pace of the school offering if some administrator says it cannot be done because of time schedules. Clearly, time schedules have to give. The same thing is true of classroom instruction. A very large number of teachers and especially of school administrators have noticed that whole-class instruction, which has been condemned by observers of education ever since the Renaissance, goes right on because of the way the school is organized. While Elwood Cubberly thought that the graded school was the ultimate in school organization, his successors have rejected it precisely because the grades present a series of artificial divisions and create of themselves one of the most nagging of all the educational problems—the problem of articulation.

The problem of articulation is a direct product of the way the schools are organized. Every time the school is segmented, an articulation problem is created. In many schools, to this day, the program in mathematics in grade 6 consists mainly of review "in order to get the students ready for grade 7." The program in grade 8 or 9, similarly, is too often given over to review and for the same reason—to get the students ready for the next institution our organization has created. Continuous progress is, of course, seriously impaired by these organizational breaks.

The problem is even more profound, however. There is a sense in which the typical organization of the schools makes getting through school the purpose of going to school. The requirements that arise from the need for smoothness of organization become the primary educational requirements the student must meet. For many years the reason offered for requiring plane geometry of all college-entering students, for example, was that it functioned as a useful hurdle for college entrance. What, one might ask, of the possibility that plane geometry has some intrinsic value? Sequences have been imposed on subjects in which there was no intrinsic sequence, such as the social studies, on the assumption that the higher one goes in school, the more advanced the subject matter ought to be. One must create something called "elementary" in order to have something called "advanced."

The purpose of going to school never was, of course, to go through school. The purpose was to gain an education. Our present organization confuses the one with the other, and the more sensitive students are expressing their outrage at it.

The changes in the organization of the schools, notably the nongraded school and the introduction of team teaching, have as their obvious intent making the school organization fluid enough so that it can respond to the differing needs of individual students. The fact that this has often not happened requires examination.

Changes in the organization of the school are much easier to undertake than are changes in its policies or substance. In a very large number of school districts, since 1955, organizational changes have been undertaken without changes in the substance of the offering. These changes have not responded to some need within the school; they have been intended in some cases only to obtain good local publicity and in others to help the superintendent gain a reputation as an "innovator." The widespread failure to change the substance of the offering has meant that the offering has gone unchanged and that the old baloney has simply been sliced in some new way. It is important that professional teachers recognize that the organization of the school is not the curriculum of the school and that it does not necessarily have any effect on the curriculum whatever.

Any organization is best considered as a set of constraints. The constraints of the graded school with the three-way separation (elementary, junior high, high school) that now characterizes most school districts have become more and more evident during recent years, and some attempt has been made here to indicate what they are. The more fluid organizations now beginning to appear would seem to have fewer constraints—at least of the old type. One constraint, however, of team teaching is that the teachers are compelled to cooperate, to learn to work together, to do things by committee. Where direct attention is not given to this need, team planning quickly degenerates into the planning of logistics, and matters of substance are not attended to. One constraint of the nongraded school is obviously that the student has to find some new way of orienting himself to the process of his education. In the graded school, it was convenient for him to name the grade that he belonged to, thus communicating to himself and others a shorthand for the progress he had so far made. In nongraded schools, in the absence of direct attention to the problem of student orientation, it is common for the student to invent some substitute for grade and to apply it to himself ("I am in level 1, phase 3"; "I am in Miss Blank's honors class"; "I am in the third year."). Just as an obvious constraint of the emerging curriculum, or the student-selected curriculum, is the enormous increase in the amount of time needed for planning, so the obvious constraint of the "School Without Walls" (see Chapter 3) is an enormous increase in the amount of time required for the recruiting and training of instructional personnel.

To fail to recognize these limitations in advance is to risk failure in the new organization. The fact that they have ordinarily been overlooked has already resulted in a considerable degree of cynicism about their value.

Teacher Militancy

One of the outcomes of increased urbanization has been a considerable sharpening of the functions of teacher organizations. The phenomenon of organized teachers making demands upon boards of education, negotiating contracts, using organized grievance procedures, and demanding equal representation and voting privileges with respect to many decisions previously reserved for administrators has become commonplace.

Less noticed than the phenomenon of militancy itself is the growth of a new pattern of teacher-administrator relationship, especially in the formation of large numbers of policy committees. It is very likely that in the years ahead these committees will become more directly concerned with the substance of instruction, following the present period in which "working conditions" are the main items on their agenda. The growth of this large structure of professional committees as a consequence of the negotiation of new-type contracts is an important development, the significance of which has not yet been realized. They are a new phenomenon in education. During the 20's, large numbers of committees of teachers were formed to design new curriculum guides. In that sense, the voice of the teacher was heard in curriculum making. During the 30's and 40's, the curriculum guides developed by such committees having fallen into disuse, participation of teachers as such in curriculum making assumed new forms: workshops, action research teams, study groups.

The present phenomenon has institutionalized those new forms. Whereas in the 20's the committees were carrying out tasks delegated to them by the administration, the present committees generate their own agendas. We may expect a much wider range of types of curriculum decisions to emerge from these committees during the years ahead than those that emerged from the committees of the 20's. In some school districts, it is likely that the committees' decisions will be very conservative and system-oriented, and in others they will become adventurous. Whatever their decisions, they are likely to have a binding force on what is in fact done in the schools, which was not true in any earlier time. We have passed through a very long period during which the administrators in the schools variously coerced and persuaded teachers to make changes. We are entering a time in which the power is genuinely shared, at the expense of the administrators.

DIVISION, COLLISION, AND HUMAN BEINGS

The teachers' world in the 70's of this century is more intense, more divisive, and more replete with fundamental change than has ever been true in American education. Let us consider this world in terms of its divisions and consequent collisions.

If there is one major aspect of the changed climate within which the students function, it is that they insist that schools be for people, not for the schools themselves, nor for society. To be a man is to be an intellectual, emotional, social, esthetic, spiritual, physical creature. If the students are to be listened to (and they insist upon it), it will be necessary that not only the manner of our teaching, but also its substance, deal with the whole of what it means to be a human being. It will be necessary, that is, that we justify the offerings that are made in the schools not only in terms of their relevance to society, but their relevance to the principal dimensions of humanity itself. To humanize the school, as the students demand, is not only to treat students in a humane fashion, but to offer them an education that will help them to deepen their humanity. The revolt against rationalism can be expected to run a course that finally puts together the rational and the nonrational within the human being—that is, a course in which the intellectual, emotional, social, esthetic, spiritual, and physical aspects of humanity are contained within what we do in education. The strictly intellectual approach that has characterized most of our thinking, including our thinking about social problems, was never adequate for actual problem solving. Any practicing politician knows that, and now our students know it, too. We have to learn what it means in educational terms.

The split world that we mirror to our students presents them with a problem, as it does us. The problem is How shall one remain sane, how shall one function as a whole person, in a world that demands that we take ourselves apart? The world is schizoid. We seek internal unity. To the degree that our offerings in school set students against one another, they portray the splits that we must try to end. To the degree that we portray the principal fields of knowledge as if they were dominated by authoritarian figures to be followed uncritically, once more we have deepened the split between the authorities and the rest of us.

Our view of the world as educators has to be one in which we celebrate the differences among men as well as emphasize their mutualities. Every man on earth is a human possibility for every other man on earth, provided only that he is in some meaningful contact with him and can apprehend the possibility. To take other people as possibilities for oneself is very different from taking them as somehow similar to oneself. To glory in the richness of our pluralistic heritage is very different from melting people down in a pot.

The growth of the cities and the explosion of our own population demand that we give new attention to the nature of privacy. The time has come to change the central function of the school, which was stated by the Educational Policies Commission in 1961 to be the development of rational powers.[7] *The central function*

---

[7] National Education Association and American Association of School Administrators, Educational Policies Commission. *The Central Purpose of American Education*. Washington, D.C.: National Education Association, 1961.

of the school is to provide legitimate grounds for self-respect. For one cannot be a private individual without self-respect; one cannot relate to others without self-respect. What is legitimate about self-respect is to be determined not only by one's private sense of well-being, but also by one's ability to relate to other people successfully and respectfully.

The changed position of the United States in the world demands of us, its citizens, a skill at social criticism that we either never had or have forgotten. The crisis of public opinion over the Vietnam war is in some degree a catastrophic reminder of our incompetence in this field. Even our most respected intellectual leaders have resorted to shrill outcry and empty polemic with respect to the war. Instead of analyzing our public problems and offering intellectual leadership in their solution, the intellectual press has too often resorted to mere vilification.

Our shrinking, divided world demands of us that all forms of stereotyping be considered poisonous and brought to an end. While this need was always present, it is now urgent. If we are to avoid catastrophic collisions with other peoples in the world, we have to come to terms with them in a way that is respectful not only of our own aims, but of theirs. We have notoriously failed to accept this task. Human understanding has to rise above the level of the armistice, or the negotiated agreement, or the *modus vivendi,* to the establishment of common purposes and enterprises.

The change in the subject matter offering in the schools gives us an opportunity to pursue to its human depths what has formerly been thought of as narrowly academic. For at the bottom of each of the major disciplines is the universe itself. To the degree that we continue to teach school subjects in order to get the student ready for the next phase, instead of carrying him further into himself, we shall miss our opportunity and fail to discharge our responsibility.

The school as an institution has to be devoted to human ends. It will no longer serve us well to consider the school as a form of business organization, with an input, a process, and an output. These are dehumanizing terms. A school is a place for people to grow into themselves, for a child to make himself into a man. Wherever this purpose is not central to the acts carried on in the school, the school is unworthy of continuation.

Education has to be realized as a function of the entire society, not just of some specialists within it. An interpretation of the school and its environment is required if all the rich aspects of humaneness are to become central to the school as an enterprise.

Teachers have to recognize themselves as human beings before they can recognize the humanity in others. The present period of teacher militancy is, among other things, a reaction against the dehumanizing of teaching. If the administrators and the public will not treat teachers as if they were complex human beings, the teachers will react by grasping power for themselves. Having already attained much power, teachers must now discover what it is to use the power responsibly, lest it be taken away from them by the public.

In the final analysis, the meaning of the difficult times we are in, from the teacher's point of view, is that teacher, pupil, parent, administrator, and the external world all have to be thought of as human beings in quandaries, seeking to grow, seeking to fulfill themselves. This is easy to say and difficult to do. We turn from saying it to considerations of what doing it might entail.

Chapter 2. The Criterion
and the Match

If one message comes through clearly from our consideration of the setting we live in, it is that the quality of individual life has to be central to public policy making. If the world is a long array of splits, then it is the individual who must find the means of sanity, and he has to find those means within himself. Society is schizoid; only the individual can be whole. If urbanization produces a new need for individual identity, it is not society that will confer it; each man must do that for himself. If new means for relating to other people must be found in our glob of a world, then the means must be based on individual integrity.

During the 70's, we are called upon to reinvent society and its institutions. We have to struggle free from the 19th century, however inviting that time, however seminal its inventions and conceptions. Our public triumphs—like the moon landings—have the ring of familiarity about them. They are goal-oriented engineering developments. We want more than anything to believe that we can still organize ourselves around heroes who, by their virtue, will give us the good life. We want to believe that our huge systems will serve us well, if only we will make them bigger and more efficient—this despite one catastrophic system-failure after another (such as the famous power failures of 1967, or the failure of U.S. foreign policy in Asia since 1950, or the threatened economic failure that confronts us as these words are written). We have survived to perceive the truth of Matthew Arnold's familiar injunction of a century ago:

Ah, love, let us be true
To one another! for the world, which seems
To lie before us like a land of dreams,
So various, so beautiful, so new,
Hath really neither joy, nor love, nor light,
Nor certitude, nor peace, nor help for pain;
And we are here as on a darkling plain

Swept with confused alarms of struggle and flight,
Where ignorant armies fight by night.[1]

In a time when the individual's needs and integrity have to be paramount, the policy according to which we govern the public schools requires a reversal. The entire tradition of public education has implied that the function of the schools is to supply manpower to fit society. The original intent of the American public schools was to fit people for citizenship—that is, participation in the revolutionary society of the day. From that day to this, the usefulness of the schools, the legitimacy of the schools, has been judged according to their effectiveness in supplying the kinds of people for society that society required. In these days, an illiterate is a public burden. Hence, illiteracy must be stamped out. In other times, we have taught the three R's because they are essential for basic employment. We are wholly swept up by the notion that educated people are more productive than uneducated people, that the manpower needs of the future demand more education, and so on. It is this whole view that has to go, if our society is to reinvent itself. If the social function of the individual is not to fit the system, but to redevelop it, then education to fit the system is irrelevant to his needs.

There is nothing in our tradition that supports the idea that the function of the school is to bring about individual fulfillment, the good life, or anything of the kind. In order to face the problems that lie immediately ahead of us, we are called upon to re-examine and revise the basic policy that has governed the schools from their inception. From this time forward, the central function of the school should be to make people more fully human, not to provide manpower.

Let us examine education with this criterion in mind. To do so, I suggest that we take the following paradigm as our guide:

The educator's question is: *who* shall learn *what, why, how,* in what *circumstances,* under what *governance?*

An educational decision, to be complete, must take at least these six components into account. If it leaves one of them out, the decision will fail because of its incompleteness. These questions

---

[1] Arnold, Matthew. "Dover Beach." *The Concise Treasury of Great Poems.* (Selected by Louis Untermeyer.) Garden City, N.Y.: Permabooks, 1953. p. 352.

could be asked at any time in education. The answers would differ according to the time, but we shall assert here that the questions are sufficient to the analytical task. They should fit all kinds of schools and all kinds of learning situations, including the learning by an individual and learning by groups of people. In using them as our guide, we shall, in each case, compare our present practice with what is required of us by the times ahead.

WHO SHALL BE EDUCATED?

At present, in the United States, almost everyone who is physically able to do so goes to school between the ages of approximately 6 and 16. Before age 6, only a select group of those children who are in school districts that provide kindergartens and nursery schools may be given a formal education. After age 16, a large proportion of the students drop out of school and go to work; a few of them to return to school later on a part-time basis. Since the dropouts select themselves according to their social class and racial membership, we may regard their attendance as less a function of their desires than of their upbringing and place in society. A larger portion (approximately 70 percent) of our boys and girls are in school at age 17 and 18 than is true anywhere else in the world. But, by that age, we have already lost from formal education approximately 30 percent of the population.

Such a situation is seriously inadequate, if the needs of the future are to be met. Self-discovery and self-realization and the making of a good life are lifelong enterprises. Education—deliberate education—also needs to be a lifelong affair. That's why Henry Adams called his life an education. The only answer to the question, "Who shall be educated?" suitable for the 70's and beyond is "Everybody. All the time." Of course, such a policy places severe strains on our present practices with respect to how people learn and the circumstances under which education shall be carried forward. But we shall come to that. For the moment, it is sufficient to point out that our old ideal of universal lifelong education will no longer be denied. Either it will be done deliberately through some modification of our present framework of education, or it will be done by extra-educational agencies and groups. Indeed, it is already being done by such groups in large measure (see the subsequent section on *Governance*).

WHAT SHALL BE LEARNED?

Curriculum I

There are always three curriculums operating in a school. Curriculum I is the formal academic offering, plus those cocurricular activities that are planned. It consists in the main of school subjects, occasionally organized on a broad fields basis, more frequently organized around the disciplines they represent. The main purpose of the school as it stands is to conduct this formal offering in as palatable and meaningful a fashion as possible. By *palatable* we generally mean that subject matter shall be offered in a way that is understandable to the student and pleasant to study. By *meaningful* we ordinarily mean that the application of the subject matter to the real world shall be evident.

By and large we know more about how to make subject matter palatable than we know about how to make it meaningful. It is easier to invent an arithmetic game than it is to make it evident that arithmetic helps one grasp the world in some meaningful fashion.

Most of the history of curriculum development in the United States has to do with curriculum I. Historically, we have tried various approaches to palatability and meaningfulness. The project method, beginning in 1918 and having a long and honorable history, was one such approach. It had at least a threefold meaning: (a) it sought to provide methods that made the learner active; (b) it sought to deal with real problems (i.e., "meaningful" content); (c) it sought to integrate subjects, to the end that students would learn that they had to use many subjects to solve real problems. The project method led quickly to the development of the unit of work in the 20's; it was incorporated in the Progressive Education movement; it later led to the development of cooperative procedures in learning or cooperative planning of the curriculum by learners and teachers.

It is interesting to note that neither the project method nor its successors seriously attempted to deal with self-fulfillment by the student as the primary and major goal of the educational enterprise. So viewed, the project method and its descendants do not match our criterion. It may well be that in the future we shall continue to make extensive use of the methods associated with the project curriculum, but its intent, which was social, will require substantial revision if it is to match the criterion of making people more fully human—more fully themselves—that is set up by our analysis of the current state of affairs and our projection of the likely state of affairs in the 70's and beyond.

With respect to school subject matter, it is necessary to acknowledge the importance of the reform, which we shall here call "the disciplines proposal," that has been in full development since the 50's.[2] It is this proposal that led to the reforms in the teaching of science and mathematics, and to a lesser degree, reforms in other academic offerings. The proposal, in brief, is that school subjects shall represent the disciplines on which they are based by seeking to teach the modes of thought that characterize these disciplines. In these modes of thought are to be found significant ways of learning. To put it succinctly, the way of knowing in a discipline is also a way of learning it. To learn physics, one learns to think like a physicist. To learn history, one learns to think like an historian.

The disciplines proposal has a number of important advantages. For one thing, it successfully brings to an end an old dispute between the generalists and the specialists in education, who find it possible in this proposal to come together around the concept of an active learner, where pursuit of the subject matter is a prominent goal of the teaching itself.

Another important advantage of the disciplines proposal is that the subject matter is presented as if it were reasonable—that is, as if a student could derive the subject matter from reasoning processes, instead of having to accept it as arbitrarily given. The invitation to reasonableness as put forward by the new curriculum of the 50's and 60's has had a revitalizing effect on the academic offering, and it presumably will continue to do so. It matches our criterion, in its own way, by respecting the student's intellectual development and by giving him means for grasping more of the world than he could without such learning. It promises to free him from slavish dependence upon intellectual authority and in all of these ways promises to contribute to his self-fulfillment.

There is yet another very important advantage to the disciplines proposal, often overlooked. At the bottom of each discipline is a set of concepts of great generative power. These generalizations are the ordinary vocabulary of the educated. They serve to bring

---

[2] The material that follows is restated and expanded somewhat in Chapter 3, no. 6 (pp. 52-54). See also "The Subject Matter Revolution," Chapter 1, pp. 14-17.

order out of the buzzing confusion of the world and convey much greater power to the individual who possesses them than he would have without them. Concepts like *inverse ratio,* from mathematics, are applicable in many nonmathematical domains. So are concepts like *tension, composition, esthetic surface*—all from the fine arts. The same may be said of the concepts *interaction, properties of objects, systems,* and *ecosystems,* all from one of the elementary science programs of the 50's and 60's. Obviously, the concepts *fact, legend,* and *myth* from the field of history have the same generative quality.

It is worth stressing that those who possess these concepts have more autonomy, and are hence freer to govern themselves, than are those who do not have them. They are hard won, these ideas, but they are worth it.

However, the disciplines proposal doesn't do everything. It does not of itself integrate knowledge, nor does it deal very effectively with the need for "meaningfulness." Perhaps more importantly still, the disciplines proposal connotes a cool, detached, objective version of what it is to be a human being, precisely at a time when it is evident that our youth, at least, want knowledge to be hot, personal, and involved—which brings us to curriculum II.

Curriculum II

Curriculum II, sometimes called the "latent" curriculum, has to do with the nature and function of authority in life, the problems of participation in the decisions that make one's own life, and in general with social development. This is the curriculum that intrudes upon curriculum I all the time, especially in these days of student unrest. It is safe to say that, at present, only in kindergarten and the primary grades is curriculum II given its due. It is exceedingly rare (though we shall offer some examples of it later) for curriculum II to be given direct attention in the upper grades and secondary schools. When a kindergarten or primary teacher draws children's attention to the need for rules to govern the microsociety of their classroom, he is dealing with curriculum II. When teachers draw children into cooperative planning of the curriculum, when they set up working committees for students to get jobs done, and in general when they put the responsibility for the conduct of the minisociety of the school in the hands of the student, they are carrying on curriculum II.

Student government in the high school is supposed to deal with curriculum II. However, it has been confined to essentially trivial matters. Only very recently have students questioned this arrangement. Some of them have thrown out student government as trivial and irrelevant. A few have arranged matters so that the students participate directly in the major decisions that operate the school. In all these ways, curriculum II is (or is not) being treated in the schools. By and large, however, we have to admit that curriculum II is left latent.

During the years ahead, direct attention should be given to curriculum II. Since the questions of the relationship of the individual to authority and the participation of the individual in inventing social structures are so central to the purposes of curriculum II, direct efforts should be made to deal with them. At the high school level, seminars on the nature and function of authority would make good sense. At least one high school does carry on a seminar on education, which is sensible.

A drastic overhaul of the social studies curriculum throughout the schools is called for by the criterion of self-fulfillment. Man is, among other things, a social animal. To be human is, among other things, to be social. (It is also much more than that.) Why shouldn't we develop social studies programs that take the possibility of society and the nature of its structures and the questions of social change as central? This is not the place to undertake an elaborate critique of the social studies—that has been well done by others—but it is important to recognize that at the very point where we have provided a curriculum offering that ought to deal with the social nature of human existence, it fails to do so. Some of our problems with law and order would disappear if people knew more about the nature of law. Instead of learning that the policemen are "neighborhood helpers," shouldn't children come to understand that a policeman is basically a law-enforcement officer? Shouldn't children be consistently confronted with the possibility of government? It is said that our cities are ungovernable. If that is so, certainly the students in the schools should understand why it is so, for they will have to participate in its ungovernability and in the restructuring of the government. The lack of reality of the social studies curriculum is one of the most striking features of our present scene. Here is precisely where curriculum II ought to be offered in a deliberate fashion.

Curriculum III

Curriculum III is a curriculum in self-awareness and in self-development. If curriculum II deals mainly with the social aspects of what it means to be a human being, curriculum III deals mainly with the private aspects of what it means to be human. As things stand, we do next to nothing with curriculum III. We have guidance officers who are charged with this responsibility, but their failure to discharge it is notorious. What is required is a whole array of experiences the function of which is to help each student to discover himself as a person, to develop legitimate grounds for self-respect, to develop satisfactory answers to the universal question, "Who am I?"

As things stand, we deal with these questions only on a crash or crisis basis. When a student gets into enough trouble, somebody may sit with him long enough to help him carry on the process of self-discovery. For most students—95 percent of them—such experiences are rare or nonexistent. Their contacts with the overburdened guidance counselor are essentially trivial in character, and in any case, they are fleeting and rare.

The match between the need and existing practice in this area is extremely poor. To bring about a match between the criterion and current practice, at least two kinds of changes would be required: (a) a broadening of the guidance function to include the search for self-awareness and a broadening of the concept of guidance so that all teachers carry on this function, and (b) a reconstruction of certain aspects of school subject matter so that curriculum III could be pursued. Here, I refer especially to the teaching of the arts.

While the teaching in elementary school art often fulfills some of the demands of curriculum III, it is not primarily construed that way. Why not take the arts the way they are supposed to be taken—that is, as modes of personal statement and personal experience? And why is it that the arts stop with the junior high school for most students? And how is it that literature is not taught as literature at the elementary level, and that at the secondary level it is taught primarily as literary history or as "self-expression?" In the field of literature, our pedagogical tradition serves us very badly indeed. Literature came into the public school curriculum as a means toward gentility, not toward self-awareness. It has been carried on in the shadow of college literature departments, but with the injunction that the literature presented to the young be "simple" and traditional. Here, especially, wholesale reform is called for if we are to meet the challenge of the future at all adequately.

Experience of the Real World

One of the consistent demands of the future is that the schools be directly resonant with the world as the world really is. Our tradition is that the world shall be set up in school as an array of artifically contrived subjects, each of which represents an intellectual approach to the world. But the world does not function in the terms of the intellectual approaches to it. These approaches are useful for analysis, but they do not themselves correspond to reality. Reality does not come in the packages represented by the traditional academic disciplines. Solutions to the crime problem are not to be found in any single discipline, nor to the problems of pockets of hunger and poverty, our century of wars, the grinding urbanization of our time, or any of the others. The daily news is very far from academia.

If the school is to be resonant with its times, it is necessary that the times be allowed to speak in their own ways in the educational enterprise. Historically, the response of the educators to this problem was contained in the core curriculum, which sought to deal directly with social problems. But the core curriculum was also burdened with the task of presenting "fundamental" subject matters, a burden it could not support. During the years ahead we can easily conceive of two parallel versions of curriculum I. One of these would be based on the academic disciplines, including the arts. The other, parallel to the first, would be based on the problems of society and of individual meaning. It would not be sensible, given our experience with this kind of thing, to delay until the secondary school the development of a curriculum dealing with real problems. The problem-centered curriculum and the academic curriculum should start immediately upon entrance in school, each being carried on in ways suitable to the life space of the students involved and carried on continually until formal education ceases.

One aspect of the confrontation of the school with external reality is often overlooked: the relationship of school to real work—real, productive work. If the school is to deal more thoroughly with reality than it has in the past, then the reality of work must be allowed to enter into schooling from the beginning. The child labor laws and compulsory attendance, those twin enactments of the 19th century viewpoint, are probably dysfunctional now. There is every good reason for young children to begin the process of being productive in the world as early as they are capable of doing so. There is no reason to suppose that because they are being productive, they are therefore being exploited. Work experience for young children, which is clearly mandated by these times, could be kept under control of the educational authorities in such a way as to ensure its educative value. But to deny children the opportunity to take part in the real world is to portray to them an irreal version of childhood—a version that is out of step with our times. A direct relationship between the world of work and the world of education needs to be established early in the game and continued throughout its duration. If we are to respond to Dewey's old injunction that education be life, not preparation for life, we should take at least this one small step, making the necessary changes in the law.

WHY SHOULD EDUCATION GO ON?

To speak of the why of education is to refer to the values, goals, and objectives of the enterprise.

If education is to be humane, the first thing we must acknowledge about the why of it is that the students' answers to this question are the main answers. If a student cannot give a good answer to the question of why he is studying what he is studying, he probably should not be studying it. Here are some bad traditional answers: "I am studying it in order to please the teacher," "I am studying it in order to get on to the next stage of schooling," "I am studying it because my parents expect me to," "I am studying it in order to get a high grade," "I am studying it because I have to." We propose here that whenever the child can give no better answer than one of these to the question, "Why are you studying what you are studying?" he probably should not be studying the subject at all.

The better answers have always been on our minds: "I am studying it because it's interesting," "I am studying it because I can learn to be a better person if I know it," "I am studying it so I can know something better," "I am studying it because it is fun." Generally speaking, we hope students study things because they come to a deepened sense of themselves and the world as a result. It is simply astonishing that we have allowed the organization and traditions of schooling to overlook this value.

Any teacher has four kinds of goals in mind for his students vis-à-vis the subject matter he is teaching: that they shall understand it, value it, have confidence in their ability to learn it, and persevere in it independently. These goals—understanding, value, confidence, and perseverance—need to guide our efforts at valuation, as well as our efforts at instruction, if the schools are to be humane. If one of them is overlooked, the student is likely to be studying for the wrong reasons. It is not sufficient to set up behavioral objectives for the teaching of subject matter that overlook these goals. The purpose of studying subject matter is not to learn a skill alone, it is to learn the skill as instrumental to something of value. Yet we continue to offer subject matter in school as if the subject matter had intrinsic value that is immediately evident to the student.

We suggest that the concept "readiness," which has come under such profound attack in recent years, be revived but redefined. Readiness to study something will have been achieved when the student can see the value of studying it, has developed confidence in his ability to undertake it successfully, and is disposed to persevere in it. (Obviously, perseverance is a function of value. The more valuable anything is, the more likely we are to persevere in its attainment.)

These goals amount to a stringent set of criteria to be applied to subject matter. Suppose we apply them to reading. What they imply is that if a student cannot see the function of his learning to read, he should delay his attempts to learn until he can. A good many of the reading problems we face probably arise from a combination of low valuing and low confidence. Some of them arise from a failure of understanding. The latter happens when we present reading simply as a decoding effort, in which the code is arbitrary and somewhat forbidding in character. It is quite possible that our present widespread concern with reading methods is misplaced. Children learn to read in all kinds of ways, provided they intend to.

The most notorious violation of these standards occurs in the teaching of mathematics. We do very little to encourage children to think that mathematics has instrumental value in the world. We offer all kinds of devices to trick them into doing something that is of itself somewhat intriguing. But the tremendous attrition in mathematics knowledge, once school has ended, testifies to our failure to teach children either to value the subject or to have confidence in their ability to persevere in it. The only widely taught skill other than mathematics that probably has a greater attrition rate is piano playing.

HOW SHALL STUDENTS LEARN?

It's perfectly possible to teach without anyone's learning anything. Suppose that someone were busy teaching by television, but didn't know that the camera had been turned off. Would one say that he was not teaching? It would be more sensible to say that he was teaching, but that nobody was learning. The same thing happens in classrooms all the time. Teachers teach, but many students fail to learn. Probably the greatest difference between professional teachers and amateur teachers is that professional teachers have an adequate theory about the learning being carried on by the students before them.

Historically, we have offered subject matter, but we have not helped students to learn it. We speak, quite properly, of the curriculum as the *offering* in the school. In the main, we leave it to the students to consider how they are to pick up the offering. Relatively little attention has been given to the teacher's role in the students' learning. We have to recognize that everything we do as teachers connotes some kind of learning behavior on the students' part. When we lecture, the student is supposed to sit and listen, perhaps to take notes, perhaps to carry on some kind of internal dialogue with us. When we give students assignments to be carried on outside of class, the form of the assignment dictates the learning behavior the student is supposed to carry on.

The most highly organized attention to students' learning behavior has been given by the constructors of workbooks and the constructors of programed instruction. It's interesting that neither in workbooks nor in programed instruction is very much use made of memorizing as a method. Yet memorizing is the primary learning method applied by students, when left to their own devices. Memorizing has served them well. Memorizing is a form of detailed imitation, the means through which most of the earliest learnings in life are actually undertaken. We do very little in school to contradict the power of memorizing as a method. Most students learn that the most certain way of passing most of the tests we give is to memorize the text or what the teacher has said and to give it back. Very rarely do we actually test reasoning. Very rarely indeed do we actually ask students as a criterion performance to take new data, form them into some coherent whole, and let us see the whole. Despite all our hopes and claims to the contrary, we continue to give more weight to the student's ability to give back facts out of context than we do anything else. Surveys of elementary students' preferred subjects have repeatedly shown that they prefer mathematics and spelling to social studies and reading, perhaps because in the case of mathematics and spelling the learning method and the tests are so obviously related to the objectives of instruction. It is interesting that we have turned over the formal testing in reading to professional test makers and that our testing in social studies consists essentially of keeping work samples, not of conducting formal evaluative exercises.

To humanize the school would be to put the learning method in the hands of the learner. While we have talked for generations about "learning how to learn," we have done little or nothing about it. During the 70's and beyond, we may expect the students to demand that we—or somebody—do more about it. One of the effective, and humanizing, kinds of approaches to this task is to ask students to teach each other. Another is to increase dramatically the amount of independent work we ask students to carry on. Nobody knows very much about school learning methods, in any scientific sense, but teachers know a great deal about it in terms of the conventional wisdom and lore of education. If students are asked to teach each other, the teacher can function as a resource person on learning method. If students are trying to memorize when they ought to be trying to reason or structure information, the teacher can at the least call to their attention the irrelevance of their method to their objectives and at most suggest ways of proceeding. The same is true with respect to independent work. "Learning how to learn" probably ought to become the focus of deliberate attention in the schools of the 70's. "How to study" should become as central to formal education as "how to read" or "how to understand scientific data."

IN WHAT CIRCUMSTANCES SHOULD LEARNING TAKE PLACE?

The traditional classroom is being supplemented these days by a wide variety of alternative educational environments: learning teams, teaching teams, independent work, street academies, "open schools," and so on. The basic circumstances under which learning is undertaken are much more various now than they were as recently as 10 years ago.

Perhaps the most convenient way to think of the circumstances that promote a humane approach to schooling is to think of each of them as a setting in which human beings are to undertake learning. What is the basic role of the student in a class of 30 with a teacher in the front of the room? His basic role is to be passive and to take his turn. What is the basic role of the student in a learning team, in which he and three or four other students are to teach each other something? His basic role is that of the teacher. But since all teachers know in their bones that the best way to learn anything is to try to teach it, perhaps learning teams will often be more desirable than whole class situations.

What of the possibility of a variety of teachers? During the 60's, team teaching as a way of presenting a variety of teachers gained considerable vogue. The idea is capable of very considerable extension. It would, perhaps, be carried to its logical conclusion if we said that the basic circumstances for education are contained within the community as a whole, not within the school itself. Let us explore this idea briefly.

One of the basic characteristics of being human is that each of us is a variety of persons and that among us we are also a variety of persons. To the degree that the educative process calls upon us to act out all the varieties we are, the process presumably is more pervasive and has greater impact. Let us therefore consider the possibility that in the future the entire community— not just the schools—shall be thought of as the educator. Let us take the schools to be specialized institutions, relating to the entire community. Let us cause the expenditure of funds for education to reflect this situation: less money for school buildings, more money for the educative community.

What we are imagining here is an education in which the students carry on a very large proportion of their educative activities at locations in the community where special resources are available: the hospital, the police department, industries, distributive institutions (restaurants, stores, and the like), coordinative activities (such as the telephone company), and so on and on. The school, if a large amount of the student's basic education were carried on in these other places, would become an educational coordinating institution. Its basic function would be to administer certain unique facilities (library, laboratories, guidance facilities), and the teacher would become mainly an educational diagnostician. Students would not go to school unless there was some good reason for them to be there. They would go to many places in addition to the school. Education would take place by appointment, much as hospital treatment takes place by appointment. Like the hospital, the school would have an intake procedure, a referral procedure, certain specialized facilities, and a system for excluding people who have been treated successfully or who don't need what it offers.

A great deal of educational activity would be undertaken by the student working alone, perhaps with programed instruction devices, film, simulations, and of course the library (considered as a retrieval system). A great deal of his activity would consist of attempts on his part to produce something of merit: an essay, an object, a system, a service, an idea, an art object.

The circumstances under which education would take place, if this idea were carried out, would be as various as the community itself. When the community did not have the facilities available for students to undertake certain kinds of activity, they would go to other communities, using local funds to pay the way. In the community I live in, for example, there is one of the few excellent stained glass studios in the country. Obviously, the studio should be used by students in the course of their art work. As things stand, this is impossible; the people who operate the studio are busy. They cannot take the time away from their work to instruct large numbers of students in the art of stained glass. If, however, students could arrive with convertible scrip that the owners of the stained glass studio could later turn in to the appropriate educational authority for reimbursement, perhaps they would add somebody to their staff to carry on the necessary educational activity with students. It is not suggested here that the community as educator be asked to carry on its educative activities as a matter of voluntary, free, goodwill offerings. It is suggested, rather, that the circumstances for education be taken seriously and formally, with the necessary costs defrayed as they are defrayed now, through tax revenues.

UNDER WHAT GOVERNANCE?

No instructional decision is complete unless the question of how it shall be judged and by whom is answered satisfactorily. Many an educational innovation has failed because the question of governance was not considered.

At present, the legal structure of the schools is almost identical all over the United States. The schools are organized on a hierarchical basis, with teachers reporting to principals, who report to superintendents, who report to local school boards, who report only to the people in their communities. We maintain the fiction that education is a function of the state, but the fact is that it is a local function almost everywhere. And the tendency to make it even more local in character is very strong among us.

It is suggested that in the schools for the 70's and beyond, especially where the responsibility for education is made a function of the community as a whole, the governance be conducted in such a way as to involve the people as a whole as well as the students in basic curriculum decisions at every point.

One of the best models of such governance is in the vocational schools. For each of the principal offerings, there is a community-school governing committee, which reviews the offerings and the evaluative devices. When the review implies a change, the change is made. Even the qualifications of the teaching staff come under review. In our communities, a network of such review committees would have the effect of making the school directly responsive to the world it is in. The risk that the local committee might be too parochial could be reduced through the participation of the professional educators. Better to take this risk than to continue the present discontinuity between the schools and their communities.

*　*　*　*　*　*

We have considered here several questions concerning education, which are combined in a "who, what, where, when, why, what governance" paradigm. These questions suggest an agenda for curriculum invention. Let us turn to it.

Chapter 3. The Agenda

At this point, two ideas should be obvious: that the times we are entering make it imperative that education be concerned mainly and directly with the people to be educated, as against being mainly concerned with meeting external social needs; and that making education human will have a radical effect on our present educational practices. The purpose of this section is to explore some of the practical requirements that such a policy makes upon us. Where it is possible, we shall offer illustrations from present practice that match the requirements.[1]

From what precedes, at least a dozen practices are required, as follows:

1. Students must participate fully in the making of curriculum plans and in deciding how they shall be executed.

2. The community is the educator. Community and school must interpenetrate each other.

3. Everyone should be a constant, consistent, legitimate part of the educational enterprise: children, parents, officials, residents—everyone. Learning has to be viewed as universal and lifelong.

4. Curriculum II, *the curriculum of social experimentation* in which the nature and need for authority, for delegation, and for governance are central concerns, requires full

---

[1] In preparing this chapter, I first wrote out the required practices as they seemed to be implied by the preceding chapters. I then went, confidently, looking for examples to match the requirements. To my surprise, I couldn't find many. Perhaps this list of required practices—a list by no means exhaustive—can be thought of as an agenda for invention. Here are a dozen educational inventions in search of inventors. We shall have to reiterate here several ideas already explored in Chapter 2, in order to make these recommended agenda items as "free standing" as possible.

and deliberate attention, in its own terms, in the educational enterprise.

5. A parallel curriculum needs to be constructed, in which one part is a prestructured academic curriculum and the other emergent and real-life oriented.

6. The disciplines offered in formal education have to be seen as contributing to the general education of students.

7. Man the social creature has to be treated as such in the curriculum. A new social studies curriculum is needed, in which the nature and possibility of society is the central content.

8. Curriculum III, *the curriculum of self-awareness and self-realization,* requires universal application and attention. The function of guidance in the schools requires reconception; its availability must be greatly increased.

9. Literature and the arts, the most universally humane of the school offerings, require substantially increased attention; they also require reform, to the end that their humane meanings become their main meanings.

10. Participation in the real world in the form of productive work should be a part of the entire educational experience, early and late. Such work should be rewarded in the usual social ways: with money, recognition, acceptance into work-related groups.

11. Study skills should be put in the hands of the learner, to the end that he become equipped with a repertoire of such skills, with knowledge about their appropriateness for various learning tasks.

12. A variety of teaching styles, planned for the purpose, should be made available to learners from the beginning of their formal education.

This list does not exhaust the implications of the criterion of humaneness when it is applied to organized education, but it will serve as a start. In the following pages, illustrations of these practices will be offered in every instance where they were found. Where they have not been found, an attempt will be made to illustrate what they might be like. The reader will add to this list of needed practices. He will know of illustrations we did not find, too.

1. STUDENT PARTICIPATION IN CURRICULUM PLANS

The idea that students should participate in the planning of the curriculum is, of course, not new. During the 30's, when the unit of work became a widely used curriculum strategy, it was common for students to participate in the selection of the experiences they were going to undertake. The cooperatively planned unit of work, however, never got past the junior high school except during the days of the core curriculum. It is rare to find a core curriculum in a secondary school today. It was common, however, for students to take part in the planning of the curriculum in the lower primary grades of the elementary school and in the kindergarten. Today's college students probably have forgotten it, but they themselves are likely to have taken part in curriculum planning when they were little children. (Is that why they think they should in college?)

It is the personal meaning of the curriculum that concerns us when we think of humanizing the school. To the degree that a student can see the purpose of his work, it is *his* work. To the degree that he cannot see the purpose of his work, he is doing somebody else's bidding and therefore somebody else's work. In order for a student to see the purpose of his work, it is essential that he participate in planning it in detail, including especially the planning of the ways that the work is to be carried out. It does not follow that we are putting the planning of the curriculum in the hands of children, with the teacher as a kind of broker or witness. What is meant is that the teacher and the students will collaborate in the selection and planning of the undertakings that they carry on in school.

Now, such collaboration takes much time as well as much skill. Students are not accustomed to planning their educational experiences. Any teacher knows that planning is a painstaking affair. To draw students into it is to move the planning of the curriculum into a central place in the curriculum itself. That is precisely what is proposed here. If it be objected that children cannot plan for something they don't know—that students can't plan a mathematics curriculum when they don't know mathematics—let it be answered that planning is a way of knowing. There is no reason, even in such a textbook-bound subject as mathematics, why students shouldn't page ahead in the book and get some notion of what a course includes before they begin it, thus being in a position to participate in the planning of it part by part. We select mathematics as an example precisely because the attrition in mathematics is among the most shocking phenomena of contemporary education. To take students through a subject step by step, the students never knowing what the next step will be, is to treat them in the most authoritarian and least humane fashion possible. Yet that procedure is at the heart of the tradition of teaching mathematics.

Not only is it true in mathematics. It is true in many another of the secondary school academic subjects.

There are two approaches to the solution of this problem in practice. One of them was classically called the "emerging curriculum." In this approach, planning went on constantly. The assumption was that what should come next ought to grow out of what is going on now. But in order for that to happen, it is necessary to plan each step as it is taken. While the students will not know how the course is going to turn out (and the teacher won't either) the constant examination of purpose offers an opportunity to make purposefulness central to classroom work.

The other approach is the cooperative planning of large blocks of work, with subdivisions of it laid out and assigned to varying groups in a classroom—a process that is entirely familiar to elementary school teachers.

Perhaps the most helpful suggestion we can make is that secondary school teachers turn to their elementary school colleagues and see what they can find out about the process of cooperative planning in the primary grades. As things stand now, the most effective work of this kind is being done in the kindergartens and at the last stages of graduate education. For most of the time in between, students have to hang on the teacher's words in order to know what's going to happen next. A good deal of the youthful challenge arises from this dependent, and essentially inhumane, relationship.

Examples

It is interesting that we found very few examples of cooperative planning at the secondary school level, when we went looking for them. They no doubt exist in many places, especially in such courses as Problems of Democracy, perhaps in studio art courses, and to some degree in athletic coaching. However, the best examples would appear to continue to be at the lower elementary school level, where the practice is not at all uncommon.

The one prominent missing element in cooperative planning practice as it exists is in the participation of the students in laying out the methods of work they are themselves to use. While in an old-fashioned unit of work, students would decide in committees who was to do what and how it was to be done, it was and is uncommon for a teacher to call their attention to the methods of work they are using and to open up additional methods with them. If a student is to know why he is doing what he is doing, he has to know why he is doing it the way he is doing it.

2. THE INTERPENETRATION OF THE COMMUNITY AND THE SCHOOL

The time is almost at an end when we can treat the school as a special institution, with its special little world that students enter each day and leave in mid-afternoon. For a school to be humane, all that it means to be human must be a part of the school, and that means that the reality of the world must be a part of the reality of the school. Before we had the long years of compulsory schooling, children learned through participation in the real world fully as much as they learned in school, and both kinds of learning were equally honored.

It is easy to look back nostalgically to a time a hundred years ago or more (for example, during John Dewey's childhood) when schooling was a more or less incidental part of growing up. In an essentially agrarian society, the community was the educator. The excessive formalism of the schools of those days could be tolerated in a society that did not depend on the school to do what people assume it should do now.

It's interesting that it's necessary to reach back to agrarian America to find a situation that looks viable from this point of view. The models available to us do indeed seem to be models of a more or less disorganized or primitive society. The anthropologists point out that what we call primitive societies take education as a function of society as a whole. In a very much more sophisticated way, interpenetration of the school and society is precisely what is happening in the most rebellious of our black slums. The blacks, having concluded that the school is inhumane, seek to enter it directly.

The idea that the community is the educator is not strange where the school is taken to have failed in its mission to offer a complete education.

> The city is a teacher, Plutarch said, and everyone who has lived in a city knows why. Within its few square miles of glass, steel, and concrete are concentrated the greatest works of commerce, art, government, and entertainment. Its boundaries—particularly in the case of the American city, with its roots in a hundred different nations—encircle the cultures of an astonishing variety of national, religious, and ethnic groups.
> Each of these facets of the city offers its own lesson. But the kind of lesson you learn depends on where you sit in the classroom.[2]

Examples

There are several examples of the school and the community interpenetrating each other. Perhaps the most fully developed example is in the Parkway School in Philadelphia, where there is literally no school building, the students carrying on almost all of their educational activities in the existing community institutions, public and private. The Parkway School is still too new to be described or appraised in detail. However, it is significant that the number of applicants for teaching in the school and for membership in the student body greatly exceeds the number of available places.

At P.S. 9 in New York City, the assistant principal, Helen Hanges, has brought in between 30 and 40 parent volunteers to assist in the tutoring of the children of this bilingual population.

At the Murray Road School, an experimental secondary school in Newton, Mass., the number of courses given by parent volunteers greatly exceeds the number given by the employed school staff, and it is common for students to meet in the homes of these volunteer teachers.

However, the central idea of interpenetration is that the community shall enter into the schooling and the schools shall enter into the community in some meaningful fashion. The most fully developed existing program, as has been said, is represented by the new Parkway School. Plans have been proposed for an even

---

[2] Howe, Harold, II. "The City as Teacher." *The Schoolhouse in the City.* (Voice of America Forum lectures, edited by Alvin Toffler.) Washington, D.C.: U.S. Information Service, 1969. p. 9.

more thoroughly integrated community-school relationship. The National Educational Associates for Research and Development (NEARAD) prepared a plan for the schools of Compton, Calif., which was focused on the development of early work experience for secondary school students, but in which the activity carried on in school would grow directly out of the problems encountered by the student when he tried to do productive work in real work situations. This plan, however, was never brought to reality.

Another example within this same broad area is the well established cooperative vocational education plan, widely practiced in American urban school districts. Students hold a job and go to school part time. Sometimes there is some relationship between the employer and the school. Of course, it is not uncommon in vocational secondary schools and in vocational schools proper to bring employers directly into the making of the curriculum. Although few cities have done as much as Dayton, Ohio, where in its John Patterson Cooperative High School all the students participate in cooperative vocational education, there are many current examples of good cooperative programs. Tucson; Richmond, Va.; and Miami come to mind immediately. In fact, the whole state of Florida receives high marks for its efforts on behalf of disadvantaged youth, where cooperative vocational programs begin at the junior high school level.

However, such existing plans, good as some of them are, do not represent the kind or level of interpenetration that is called for by our basic criterion. The main meaning of the criterion of humaneness as it is applied to the interpenetration of the school and community is that the reality of the community and the reality of the school shall become parts of one another. The practice of sending representatives from one institution to the other does not fully meet the criterion. It would be met if, as apparently is the case at the Parkway School, students carried on their education in the midst of actual reality. It would be met, that is, if we took the community as the educator and if we saw the city basically as a learning environment. This has not yet happened except in scattered instances.

3. UNIVERSAL PARTICIPATION IN EDUCATION

Closely related to the idea that the community is the educator is the idea that everyone in the community is some kind of teacher and should be directly involved in the organized educational enterprise. If the school is to become humane, it is necessary to recognize that learning is a part of the basic human condition. In our efforts to end the separation between school and life, we can do no less than to bring into the formal educational enterprise all the people in the community. If education is to be universal and lifelong, the idea that there is a period of formal education that comes to an end must itself come to an end. The difference between the education of the young and the educational activities carried on by the adults would be a matter of degree and time, not of "formal" and "informal" approaches. Our present habits, which are very deeply ingrained in us, relegate the child to the school and have him emerge from it into life. It is precisely this kind of distinction that the criterion of humaneness requires us to bring to an end.

Examples

The best examples of universal lifelong education are to be found in primitive tribes, where everybody is a teacher and everybody is also a learner. The only examples inside the United States that we have been able to find are in some hippie communes and other utopias, where the conditions of primitive tribal life have been in some sense reconstituted. When all the people living in a neighborhood near Harvard University decided to have cars prohibited from their alley so that it could be turned into a mall, and when they all took on the education of the young children living in their new mall, something approaching universal participation in education had been achieved, even if only in a limited fashion. In its original form, Berea College had this quality—an educative community was created in which all kinds of activities were thought of as educative (including the making of art objects and useful tools, and also including the raising and preparation of food). Something like the educative community has been created at other colleges, such as Goddard and Antioch.

In each of these instances, it has seemed necessary to create an independent community, if universal participation in education were to be achieved. Prominent on the agenda of innovations to be created would be the development of a way of extending these somewhat isolated and precious examples to include the heterogeneous populations of existing nonindependent communities. In order that this be done, it probably will be necessary for us to abandon the utopian quality of such communities, to compromise with the ideologies that ordinarily characterize them, and to take learning in all its forms, with all its mistakes, as the reality with which we wish to deal.

4. FULL ATTENTION GIVEN TO THE CURRICULUM OF SOCIAL EXPERIMENTATION

We have called the curriculum of social experimentation "curriculum II," in order to give it full recognition along with curriculum I (the academic curriculum) and curriculum III (the curriculum of self-awareness).

Full attention to curriculum II is demanded by the criterion of humaneness precisely because it is in curriculum II that the confrontation among human beings takes place. Curriculum I, considered the exclusive curriculum of the school, connotes a puppet-like relationship between student and teacher—that is, each is the other's puppet. Curriculum I calls for role-taking by its participants. Curriculum II calls for direct engagement. It is in the thrust and parry and grope of reaching social accommodations that people can discover what it means to say that man is a social creature. It is a commonplace to say that schools are social institutions. It is not nearly so common to recognize that the version of social behavior we induce in schools is unlike any other social form. Taken as representative of the reality of social behavior outside of school, it is grotesque. What the criterion demands is that we create a real student government in the schools at all levels and that students undertake direct experimentation with public order, law, authority, and power. In the course of carrying on such experimentation, it is necessary that the students be allowed to make mistakes—even serious mistakes. In order that such activity be educative, it is essential that the students be led to think over what they have done, to draw conclusions from it, to attempt generalizing from their experience. In large measure, the school should be run by the students.

The risks associated with such a view are obvious. For one thing, students bring no knowledge or experience to curriculum II. Their groping and experimentation and mistakes will take a great deal of time—time that is now spent either out of school or studying the academic curriculum. A school that gave full attention to curriculum II would probably have to stay in session longer each day and longer each year than is now customary. Perhaps as we move toward a year-round school, we shall have room for curriculum II.

The promise of such a curriculum is obvious, also. There have been a few student-run schools, and there is ample testimony that students who go through such experience become independent and dignified, sophisticated in the arts of social discourse, and exceptionally verbal.

Examples

The most widely known example of curriculum II is in A. S. Neill's Summerhill, where the students live at the school and spend endless hours debating all aspects of school policy, including the employment and retention of teachers. The "free universities" that have appeared in a few places in the world are also examples of curriculum II in action. At the Murray Road School in Newton, Mass., students experiment constantly with the authority of the community and with the place of the teachers in it. It is a rocky road; some students "tune out," some students drop out. It is full of anxiety and tension, but there is a basic peacefulness about the school that is rare. There is an intelligence, too. For example, at Murray Road, there was a theft of money. In most schools, the staff would undertake to locate the thief and to counsel him on his behavior, meanwhile seeking restitution. The students at Murray Road didn't see it that way. They held a bake sale to raise enough money to make restitution, no doubt assuming that the thief would take part in the bake sale and that whatever punishment or advice was necessary would be contained within the social behavior of the school, thus making it unnecessary for the thief to be subjected to a direct confrontation with his accusers. He would have to accuse himself and to deal with himself in a social context created for that purpose. How much more subtle was the wisdom of the students than the usual wisdom of teachers in such cases!

Another example of the same kind is in the Experiment in Free Form Education (EFFE) in Montgomery County, Md. In this instance, the students gained permission to operate schools wholly according to their own views for a week. The endless planning and haranguing that resulted were predictable. It is hard to draw a conclusion from a one-week experiment, but the lengthy evaluation conducted by the students suggested that the principal output of the week was in curriculum II. It was evident that the students had, in the course of planning and creating their school, achieved a new dignity.

5. A PARALLEL CURRICULUM

There is nothing about the criterion of humaneness that says that organized knowledge should not be taught. We shall come to the requirements of organized knowledge a bit later. What is required is that there be a parallel curriculum in the school, one side of which deals with organized knowledge, the other side of which deals directly with social and human problems as they actually occur. Public problems like crime, inadequate housing, racism, and the relations between local and central governmental structures do not come in forms easily treated within the academic subjects, nor indeed within the academic curriculum. It is therefore necessary that they be treated in their own right, parallel to the academic curriculum.

We have experimented with something like a parallel curriculum repeatedly since 1920, when the project method was first urged upon us. It has gone by various names: multidisciplinary, project, core, problems of democracy, and so on. It matters little what it is called. It is essential that when social problems dealing with undisciplined reality are studied, the reality be dealt with. There is no point in teaching students as if their proper posture toward life were to be students of it and then expect them to transfer that kind of training to the requirements that go with participation in it.

The parallels perhaps ought to divide the student's time and attention into equal parts. We seem not to know how to reduce the amount of time currently given to the academic side of the curriculum, though we probably could reduce it somewhat. If equal time is to be given to the parallel curriculum, then more time must be found somewhere. Once more, we come to the need for an extended school day and an extended school year.

Examples

We found no examples of the parallel curriculum as described above. There are courses that seem to deal with social problems. Occasionally, the English-social studies core takes social problems as its center. The Problems of Democracy course is extremely uneven in quality as actually offered in American high schools, but it does exemplify in a highly limited fashion the parallel curriculum that is called for here. There is a series of social studies projects that focus on human relations now appearing in various parts of the country. One example is the human relations education project of western New York, funded under Title III of the Elementary and Secondary Education Act, administered through the Buffalo, N.Y., Public Schools. The program is comprehensive, extending from kindergarten through the twelfth grade, and thus begins to meet our criterion of a parallel curriculum. The same can be said of the Focus on Inner-City Social Studies (FICSS) conducted by Kent State University, including experimental units such as these: "Families in Our City" for the primary grades, "The Afro-American in United States History" prepared for grades 5, 8, and 11; "Nigeria: An African Dilemma" for grades 6 and 10; and "Minority Power in America" for grades 9 and 11. There are many examples of this sort summarized in *A Directory of Research in Curriculum Development Projects in Social Studies Education.*[3]

The trend in the newer social studies projects is toward making the social studies a parallel curriculum. One looks in vain, however, for units that deal directly with front page problems or that promise to prepare students to deal with such problems. Somehow, a combination of immediate concerns within enduring problems has to be made in such a way as to avoid the superficiality of the daily newspaper, while at the same time avoiding the remoteness of the school unit. This educational invention remains to be made.

6. THE DISCIPLINES AS GENERAL EDUCATION [4]

One of the truly significant innovations in the curriculum has been going on since about 1955 when, on the basis of funds first

---

[3] Prepared and written by the staff of the Marin Social Studies Project, Marin County Superintendent of Schools, 201 Tamal Vista Boulevard, Corte Madera, California 94925.

[4] The reader will notice that much of what is said here has already been stated in Chapter 2. It is repeated here partly for emphasis, partly to make it possible for the reader to take this chapter out of its context for use in school planning, should he wish to.

from the National Science Foundation and later from the Office of Education, the academic subjects of the curriculum were reformed so that they bear a closer correspondence to the disciplines they represent. The effect of this series of reforms has been twofold: the school subjects have been greatly enlivened; they have become more separated, one from another (see "A Parallel Curriculum" above). The concept of a general education has not so far been considered by the people who have constructed the new discipline-oriented curriculums.

I propose here that the concept of a general education through a discipline-oriented curriculum be confronted directly. If students are to feel less like puppets, it is necessary that they be drawn into the means of inquiry represented by the various fundamental disciplines their school subjects represent. It is also necessary that they see the intellectual relationships among these disciplines—that they be drawn into the ordinary discourse of the educated. Curriculum reformers apparently have not yet recognized such a possibility.

At the bottom of each of the organized disciplines is a series of concepts that apply to many domains other than those out of which the concepts arise. These concepts can be thought of as the intellectual components of a general education. General education consists of that body of fact, skill, and value that is held in common by the people in a given society. It is to be distinguished from special education in a given discipline. It is precisely the power that these concepts have to grasp great reaches of the reality that makes them important for school purposes. It is proposed here that their general meaning—as well as their special meaning—be emphasized in academic education.

The concept *interaction*, for example, arises in the Science Curriculum Improvement Study at grades 1 and 2. Students learn that objects can interact by virtue of their properties. It is common for children who are exposed to this program to adopt the term *interaction* as a part of their ordinary speech. With a little help, they could see that interaction is a part of social behavior, as well as physical behavior—but they are not given such help. The concept *inverse ratio* arises in mathematics. But there are all kinds of inverse ratios in life. The concept can be applied to medicine, economics, political behavior, the arts, and so on. The concepts of *composition, esthetic surface, tension,* and *parsimony* all arise in the visual arts. They are applicable in all kinds of other domains. The concepts of *fact, legend,* and *myth* all arise in both literature and history. But they can be applied as well in science, political behavior, and so on.

Students have to be led to make such applications, however. Left to themselves, their applications will be spotty and inadequate. What we mean to emphasize here is that concepts of this kind form the ordinary language of the educated. We strongly urge the teachers of academic subjects to assist the children in seeing the general application of the fundamental concepts (the "key" concepts) of the disciplines they teach.

Examples

We found no examples of deliberate attention to generalizing the separate disciplines in the existing programs. We submit it, therefore, as being part of the agenda for invention that a humane school implies.

7. SOCIAL STUDIES FOR SOCIETY

Man is, among other things, a social creature. Some form of society is inevitable among human beings. A humane school would be centrally concerned with the basic properties of human existence, one of which is social. The central concern of the social studies has never been satisfactorily identified; we suggest the following: the main objective of the social studies for a humane school is to indicate the terms in which a society is possible. In the revised social studies, children would constantly experiment with social forms; they would become informed critics of the social forms they have inherited. The possibility of society would be examined from as many points of view as are appropriate for growing children.

The social studies programs that have existed during the past 70 years have sometimes sought this end, but too often in a confused manner. The key concepts of the social studies should be those concerned with society: the ideas of law, power, social structure, government, justice, equity, compromise and accommodation, and the like should occupy central and permanent places in such a program. The fundamental bases by which people associate themselves with one another would be under constant examination. The personal meaning of social involvement would occupy a central place. All of this and more would be necessary if the meaning of the social nature of man were to be examined in the social studies curriculum.

Examples

In the long list of new social studies programs there are a good many partial illustrations of the kind of program the criterion demands. There is no wholly satisfactory illustration, however. The programs dealing with human relations obviously deal with the fundamental basis for human association. *Man, a Course of Study* seeks to deal with the basis for building societies, from an anthropological point of view. There are history and geography courses that teach students the nature of history or geography as a discipline. Some new economics courses have the same intent with respect to economics. Examples of a politically oriented social studies course are rare indeed. The best one we have found is the proposed social sciences education framework for the California public schools, a kindergarten through grade 12 program published in 1968. The program begins with the question "What is a man?" in grade 1, proceeds through such questions as "What happens when different groups of men come in contact?" and "How is any man like no other man?" in grades 5 and 6, to studies of public decision making and law, modernization, urban life, cultural unity in a diverse population such as India, and in grade 12 "What is the effect on social policy decisions of the relationships between organizations?" One can fault this program for various reasons—but one can fault any program. The central emphasis of the program matches our criterion as closely as anything we have seen.

The development and refinement of such programs as this are very definitely on the agenda for curricular invention implied by the criterion of the humane school.

8. THE CURRICULUM OF SELF-AWARENESS

Curriculum III, the curriculum of self-awareness, has to occupy a central place in a humane school. The one universal question asked by youngsters growing up, as well as by adults, is "Who am I?" Young people, especially, search passionately for their own identities. Much of the angry rebellion among young people arises from the failure of the school to make this central question central to the school itself.

If the school were to concern itself centrally with the question of individual identity, it would have to be reformed radically. The individualization of the school turns precisely on the recognition of curriculum III as a legitimate—and time consuming—part of the stated activity of the school. As things stand, the school becomes concerned with the problems of individual identity only when something goes wrong. For the great majority of students, the school does not concern itself with this question.

In ignoring the question of individual identity, the school is true to its own tradition as a social institution. Society does not demand of us that we fulfill ourselves. Society does not put up the criterion of individual self-awareness as a requirement for social participation. A school that made self-awareness or self-fulfillment central to its meaning would have to revise its objectives fundamentally. If the present general objective of the school is to acculturate or to socialize young people so that they may function well in society, the *humane* function of the school would be to provide for students legitimate grounds for self-respect. The humane criterion requires that this be the central purpose of the school. I repeat: the central function of the school is to provide legitimate grounds for self-respect.

But there is no self-respect without knowledge of self. There can be no self-respect without self-fulfillment and self-awareness. Even the social function of the school requires self-respect, if we would but recognize it. There can be no mutual respect without self-respect—people regard others in very much the same terms that they regard themselves. The ironic proposition the schools impose is that students regard themselves as they are regarded by others—a reversal of the golden rule and an impossibility. Precisely to the degree that the students accept this injunction, they become social puppets.

To make the building of legitimate grounds for self-respect the central function of the school is to make the guidance function of the school central—not peripheral—to its operation. It is to go beyond the school's present social mandate to a new level of educative activity. It is to risk criticism from those who do not know themselves, who seek to impose their will upon the young. It is to reverse the present emphasis of school programs, one that seems to imply that what is good for the country is good for the individual. Not so. What is good for the individual is good for the country, as our forefathers knew in their bones.

A curriculum that sought to deal with the problem of self-awareness would give primacy to guidance in all its activities. With respect to guidance, as with respect to a good many other serious problems in the school, we probably have all the right slogans already. Guidance should be a function of the school as a whole. Everybody should carry on guidance. Specialized guidance competence should be made available both to deal with particularly complex student problems and also for consultation with teachers. These are elements of our conventional wisdom that have been with us for a very long time. All that remains is for us to act on them. As things stand, our performance in this area is notoriously poor. Many schools have no guidance consultants; those that do have them give them impossible loads; most teachers do not accept guidance as a part of their normal activities.

Examples

The best examples of guidance permeating the school's activities are to be found in the "open schools" that are run by students and in the emergent parallel schools in some urban centers. It is interesting that whenever the students or the community take over, guidance moves to the center of the curriculum immediately. At the Murray Road School in Newton, for example, individual discussions between students and teachers about the students' struggles with themselves are as normal a part of the daily activity as anything else. Because the school has an open schedule, such discussions can take place almost at the drop of a hat, and they do. In the EFFE School, already cited, the teachers found themselves drawn into exploratory discussions with individual students at every point in the development of the school. The students, having on their minds the constant quest for identity, found the planning of their open school an occasion for exploring themselves. The teachers, being willing to work with the individual students as well as with the large number of committees that were formed, found themselves drawn into guidance-like discussions all the time. The same sort of thing is true of the street academies and other emergent parallel schools that are appearing in the urban slums. Given the slightest chance to do so, students will take whatever resources are at hand to carry on self-exploratory activity and talk.

9. THE CENTRALITY OF LITERATURE AND THE ARTS

The most humane subjects we offer in the lower schools are literature and the arts. Our tradition in the arts is helpful; it was a laboratory-centered offering long before the laboratory approach to the teaching of the academic subjects became a widespread practice. It never occurred to the art teachers that they should teach the elements of art before they allowed students to attempt to produce anything. On the contrary, students discover their need for knowledge in the course of attempting to produce art objects. The objects are their own. The identification of the student with his own production is intimate and pervasive. The good programs (there are many of them) in art education offer an unequalled means for self-discovery and the enhancement of the fully human qualities of the human being.

Literature is, of course, one of the arts. Sadly, our traditional approach to literature has failed to recognize this on a large scale. We have tried to academicize the teaching of literature, with the result that poetry has been made into prosody and short stories and even novels into reading exercises. But to study literature in its own right is to study the human condition. The function of fiction in the world is to make endurable that which would otherwise be unendurable. There is some Macbeth in all of us, but we can't find that out directly. We would do better to read Macbeth thoughtfully and better still to perform in it and to see it performed excellently. There is some of Captain Ahab in all of us, too, but we'll never find it out if we don't get below the surface of *Moby Dick*. We have all "wandered lonely as a cloud," but we'll never know it (or never know that it is legitimate) if the poem is reduced to prosody.

In general, in school we seek to reduce literature to the dimensions of a set of directions on a cereal box. To do this is to betray the meaning of literature and to deny our students the opportunity for the discovery of the human condition, which is the central function of literature. In a humane school, the literary qualities of literature would appear at the beginning of schooling, as would the esthetic qualities of art. Both are means to self-fulfillment. Both are primary means to gaining an experience of what it means to be a human being. Our criterion of humaneness requires that they be made central to the purposes of education and therefore central to the curriculum.

Examples

Examples of good teaching in the elementary art program are numerous. It is one of the few areas that has received prolonged attention and is often very well taught. But the attrition of interest and participation in the arts between the junior high school and the senior high school is very severe and requires attention. What, one may ask, has happened to the enthusiastic participation in the arts of the junior high school students by the time they are in the tenth grade? In part, the answer is that they have been counseled away from the arts and told that the arts are a more or less trivial elective in an academic program. But this is only part of the answer. Part of the problem must be laid at the door of the secondary school art teacher, who too often sees studio art as reserved for the children with talent and thus excludes the majority.

The status of the teaching of literature in the elementary and secondary schools has changed scarcely at all during the past 50 years. There are many excellent teachers of literature, but they tend to be alone in their schools. The attitude toward literature held by the usual school administrator is, to say the very least, uninformed.

Steps toward improvement in these two areas are under way. A national program in esthetic education is under development at CEMREL, the Central Midwest Regional Laboratory, where an attempt is being made to develop curriculum materials in all of the arts, including theater and the dance as well as literature, music, and the visual arts. As this program emerges from its developmental stage, one may expect that at least the means will be available for raising our teaching in this area to a new level of humane importance.

Parallel to developments in teaching the arts is an important development in the theory of the teaching of literature, set forth in a monograph by Alan Purves of the University of Illinois, recently published by the National Council of Teachers of English.[5] For Purves, the basic phenomenon in the teaching of literature is the student's response to a literary work, and the teacher's task is to deepen and enrich this response. He therefore presents an authoritative analysis of the possible responses to literature

---

[5] Purves, Alan C. *Elements of Writing About a Literary Work: A Study of Response to Literature.* Research Report No. 9. Chicago: National Council of Teachers of English, 1968.

and offers a way of analyzing the actual responses that students exhibit. The monograph can form the basis for a new approach to the making of curriculums in literature. It also forms the basis for a fresh and highly relevant approach to evaluation of the actual responses that students learn to make. In principle, the schema fits both the elementary and the secondary school curriculums in literature.

10. EARLY PARTICIPATION IN THE REAL WORLD

A humane school would allow humanity to interpenetrate it in all its real forms. The curriculum would, therefore, provide for actual participation in the real world as it actually is, just as much as possible. One form this can take is through early and continuous work experience or participatory experience in which the school child takes a real and active part in the affairs of the nonschool world.

Of all the curriculum areas that have been both recognized and neglected for a very long time, perhaps the area of work experience is the worst. It became apparent 60 years ago that we were trifling with it, in the days of Sloyd and manual training. Recognition of its importance paved the way to industrial arts, a still neglected area, but the curriculum in this field moved further and further away from reality. Our work experience programs at the secondary school level have been directed principally to potential dropouts. The great majority of students have no contact with work as a part of their formal education, and if they do work on the side, the selection of the jobs and their experience in them is both accidental and unexamined.

If participation in the real world, in the real world's terms, were to be made a part of school, the accusation of irrelevance would melt away. Such participation, it is worth emphasizing, would be planned, sequential, but always real. The rewards and punishments that ordinarily go with real work in the world would obtain in this instance, too. When the students' work had monetary value, they would be paid. Hopefully, this would often be the case and always the case some of the time for all of the students. Where the primary reward for social participation is affiliation with a working group, such affiliation would be fostered. Where the primary reward for work is the satisfaction of doing it, as is the case in many socially oriented endeavors, the students would be accorded that satisfaction and the recognition that goes with it. No realm of real life would be excluded from the school's curriculum, provided only that it be respectable. Students would have direct experience with as broad a section of the real world as was possible for them.

The purpose of such a curricular arrangement would be that students come to recognize the relationship between reality in the external world and the simulated reality that goes on in school. Their futures are real, of course, and the curriculum would be intended to give them a taste of the reality they are moving into as early as possible. Elementary school children would participate in secondary school and in college, as well as in work activities—medicine, distributive occupations, manufacturing, service occupations, social service enterprises. The broader purpose of such curriculums would be that the student discover himself as a participant in the world.

As things stand, the schools at their best only teach children to anticipate the world, not to participate in it. The purpose of such programs would be to bring nonparticipation to an end.

There is a host of objections to such a plan. The most traditional objection is that the child labor laws forbid early work experience—but the child labor laws have probably outlived their usefulness and should be modified. Their primary function at this time is to keep young people out of the labor force, not to prevent them from being exploited. As we move into a time when adult life and adult roles will be assumed at earlier and earlier points in life, our postponement of actual work until the end of adolescence becomes more and more nonresonant with society and with the purposes of education.

Such a plan, admittedly, would be difficult to manage, but there are some examples available of strong beginnings in this direction, in which the problems of management have been solved. It would take more time than the present school year and school day allow, but the school year and the school day obviously must be extended, as we have pointed out several times.

It is very unlikely that, in its present form, the school can accommodate the early work experience and widespread participation that our criterion implies. We say to those in the present-day school that they face serious competition from parallel schools already. Those parallel schools that offer real participation in the world as a part of their official fabric will surely win out in the competition against the narrower, less rich school environment that we currently take for granted, unless gross changes are made in the present school.

Examples

One of the best known examples of early participation is in the schools of Richmond, Calif., in a program developed by Marvin Feldman when he was a teacher there. For a significant proportion of the secondary school population there, Feldman managed to work out a rich variety of participatory experiences in the world of work. While his program was not as extensive as the one proposed above, it remains one of the most ambitious steps in this direction so far undertaken. Similar programs have been undertaken in the schools of Camden, N.J., and elsewhere under the sponsorship of the Ford Foundation, where information on such programs can be obtained.

However, there are no examples so far of the universal application of such programs to the school population, and there are very few examples of early participation—that is, participation by children beginning at age 6 and 7. The Technology for Children Project, developed by the New Jersey State Department of Education in 1966-67 with support from the Ford Foundation, is one pilot program in this area. The development of such programs on a much broader scale is on our agenda for curricular invention. Meanwhile, it is worth emphasizing, such programs are gradually appearing in the unofficial parallel school system that is beginning to emerge in this country.

11. STUDY SKILLS IN THE HANDS OF THE LEARNER

We hear much these days of independent work as a requisite for the individualization of instruction, and so it is. The implication of our criterion of humaneness is that students be made competent to carry on independent work, as well as given the opportunity to do it. We propose here that an old idea be revived and developed: the idea of teaching students how to study. "Learning how to learn" is one of our more memorable slogans; it is proposed here that we act on it.

As things stand, attention to study skills is almost wholly incidental to instruction. Where teachers pay attention to it, most frequently they seek no more than that students be diligent, not that they be skillfully diligent. Most students go through school with only the slightest broadening of their repertoire of study skills. Having learned when they were infants that imitation is a useful form of learning, they go right on using this infantile approach; they also memorize. The higher forms of intellectual activity rarely receive attention in their own right from teachers, and students usually don't discover them for themselves.

What is proposed here is that the repertoire of learning skills be identified early, given deliberate attention in its own right, and incorporated into the behavior of all the children in school. Only if this is done on a large scale can independent work be carried on successfully. Only if this requirement is met will it be possible to carry on the individualization of instruction we all say we desire.

When a teacher gives an assignment, he is of course prescribing to the students a learning method. How simple it would be if he were to call attention to the learning method he is prescribing at the point of his prescription!

The contemporary literature on study skills is dominated by programed instruction. Other than this one kind of approach, little contemporary attention has been given to the matter. It is proposed that scholars in this area renew their efforts to make available to teachers disciplined and authoritative studies of the process of study itself.

Examples

We found no examples of the kind of deliberate attention to study skills that is called for here, though no doubt some teachers do give it attention. The development of the literature of the field, and the development of the practice itself, are therefore parts of our agenda for curricular invention.

12. A PLANNED VARIETY OF TEACHING STYLES

Just as there are different methods for study or different approaches to learning, so there are different approaches to teaching—a variety of teaching styles. As things stand, people who go through school are exposed to something of a variety of teaching styles, but it has been found that teaching styles tend to standardize themselves within schools and within teaching teams. If the school is to be humane in the sense that the rich variety of the meaning of the human condition is to be made available to students, then certainly the great variety of teaching styles should be a part of the learner's experience. What is proposed here is that teaching styles be identified and that the student's progress through school be planned in such a way as to expose him to such a variety. He shouldn't emerge into adult life with the assumption that there is one best way to teach—such an assumption would indeed be naive.

A variety of valid teaching styles has yet another meaning: it means that there is a variety of kinds of persons and approaches to life that characterizes teachers. Very little attention has been paid to what it means in a personal sense to be a teacher. One thing it means is that one's teaching style is a direct projection of oneself. To acknowledge a variety of valid teaching styles is to acknowledge a variety of persons who teach and to stop stereotyping teachers and teaching according to a limited notion of what valid teaching is like.

Examples

We found no examples of a planned variety of teaching styles being made available to learners while they progressed through school, though there is a growing literature about teaching styles themselves. This, too, must be considered as a part of the agenda for curricular invention.

* * * * * *

The attentive reader will have noticed that we have not included individualization as a part of the agenda. This is not an oversight. We consider individualization of instruction synonymous with the making of a humane school. All of the items on our provisional agenda have to do with individualization of instruction. If all of them, and others we have not mentioned, were put into effect, the school would become a center for individualized learning and individualized living. The individual would be recognized, and the school would therefore be humane. Individualization of instruction is, therefore, a property of the agenda as a whole and not a subordinate part of it.

Our agenda for curricular invention is not intended to exhaust the possibilities, but to indicate some of those that are most available and perhaps most urgent. Perhaps the reader of this book will wish to add to the agenda. We hope that he will wish to undertake carrying on some of the inventions we have called for.

A Closing Word:
Yes, But What Can *I* Do?

We have run out of alternatives. The school as we know it has a heritage of inhumaneness. Instead of treating students as individual human beings, we group, track, segregate, stereotype. It is not surprising that the students, learning the hidden lesson in such practices, do the same thing to one another and to their elders. Instead of treating an education as an opportunity for a child to grow into a man, we treat it as a race for grades and reflect the societal demand for competition. It is not surprising that the more thoughtful students ultimately reject the game. We have tried every approach there is to responding to society's demands as if these demands would lead individuals to a sufficient view of the good life, never stopping to question the premise.

Well, it is being questioned now. A growing number of teachers and students demand that the school be genuinely humane—that it innovate in ways that challenge some significant parts of its tradition. There can be little question that those who fail to sense the urgency of such innovation will be left behind during the decade ahead. The time for exhortation is nearly past. The time for active, widespread innovation has arrived.

Teachers have been exhorted to do this or that since the beginning of time. The difference between the professional view of needed educational reform and the lay view is that the professional does not stop with exhortation. One cannot merely propose an agenda for reform and leave it at that. The question, "Yes, but what can *I* do?" has to be answered.

Teachers in school systems try new things all the time. The picture of the rigid, backward looking, unchanging educational bureaucracy is mere caricature. The problem we face is not that of undertaking new things, for we constantly undertake new things. The problem is to get the new things into focus. The proposal here is that we focus our innovative efforts on the creation of a humane school. To do this, we have to pay attention to what has been discovered about innovative strategies that work and that don't work. We have also to consider the place in the innovative strategy of at least two groups of people: the teachers and the administrators.

INNOVATIVE STRATEGIES THAT WORK

A considerable amount of speculation about innovation has been carried on, especially during the past 10 years. We shall not review it here. Rather, we shall attempt to draw some broad lessons from it.

Innovative strategies that work have usually paid careful attention to the following components of innovation: design, the awakening of local interest and concern, local experimentation, redesign for local purposes, and a continuing process of evaluation at every step along the way.

More innovations have failed than have succeeded, if one means by success that the innovation has in fact been adopted widely. When they fail, it is typically because they have not been conceived in a comprehensive fashion. The core curriculum, for example, once widely talked about, has largely faded from the American secondary schools. Hindsight says that the failure was in the design, which was not sufficiently explicit and therefore required extensive teacher training so that the design could be made locally. Sometimes the design is well conceived, but local awareness and interest are not attended to, so that local trial is not undertaken. Some innovative strategies consist entirely of the development of local awareness and interest (through the media and much exhortation), but nothing comes of them because good public relations in the short range apparently has been their purpose. Typically, innovations are not adequately evaluated while they are being developed, and mistakes are allowed to be carried on to their logical extreme, whereupon the innovation is judged a failure. That is apparently what is happening to Project Head Start.

Educational innovation, like education itself, is carried out at the local level. The innovations that interest us, therefore, are those that are undertaken locally.

POINTS OF BEGINNING

A Single Teacher as an Innovator

On our agenda for curricular invention, there are six items which individual teachers can work on without clearance from others and without having to overturn the school system. The six items, numbered as described in Chapter 3, are as follows:

1. Full participation by students in curriculum making.
4. Building curriculum II, the curriculum of *social experimentation.*
6. Treating the disciplines as general education.
8. Developing curriculum III, the curriculum of *self-awareness.*
9. Reforming the teaching of literature and the arts.
11. Teaching students study skills, seeing to it that they "learn how to learn."

The thoughtful teacher will see opportunities to move with respect to the other elements of the agenda, of course. These six, however, are wholly within the control of one teacher in his classroom, and he could, if he wished, act alone on them.

Within one's own classroom, one is free to design and try out novel approaches. The teacher who wished to involve students in curriculum making is of course free to do so. If he hasn't tried it, we would suggest that he start with a short-range project of some kind until he gets the feel of it. Why not ask the students to plan the curriculum for one period or one week? Remember, it is important that they plan their methods of work as well as the topics to be studied. They have to plan the evaluation of the learning, or the act of planning will be incomplete.

Try it. See how much time it takes and what problems emerge. Think it over and try it again, making allowance for the problems. You will find that when students plan their own curriculum, they wind up teaching each other. They may well plan sessions for tutoring one another, for helping one another, for helping the teacher. None of these things is ruled out. In evaluating our item no. 1, it would be worth seeing whether the students feel any more responsibility for carrying out the plans well when they have made them than they do when they carry out the teacher's plans. There is some research and speculation that suggests that students view classroom work as a game in which the teacher is the antagonist, and they win the game if they get by without the teacher's penalizing them. A cooperatively planned curriculum would change the rules of the game.

The same thing is true generally of classroom innovations. One starts small both in scope and in time. One starts with a low risk of failure, or where the risk of failure can be tolerated (hence the suggestion of a short period of experimentation to begin with), one redesigns, one evaluates, and so on.

Of course, teachers would not be confined to our list of innovations that need to be invented or extended. They will have their own. We would suggest only that the innovations we undertake for the future be focused on the development of a more humane school.

We did not mention in our list, for example, the interesting development in health education for which the materials have been designed by the School Health Education Study located at the National Education Association in Washington.[1] The new program gives full recognition to the fact that man is a total being and seeks to teach students that they exist as physical, moral, intellectual, emotional, esthetic, and spiritual wholes.

Participation in Professional Activities

But a teacher need not be confined to such experimentation as he can carry on in his own classroom. He can start things up locally. He can see his administrators about the undertaking of larger scale experimentation. He can consult with his local professional organizations to the same end. He can bring to their attention the numerous materials from the divisions and departments of the NEA. He can take part in regional and national activities. He can watch out for institutes and special programs at local colleges and universities and take part in them. If he has an agenda for innovation of his own, he can comb the journals for help on specific projects.

Concerning this last, using the educational literature, an additional word is perhaps called for. Educational journals deal with everything there is, in no particular order and with rather poor quality controls. One has to search through an awful lot of dross

---

[1] For further information, write to the School Health Education Study, 1507 M Street, N.W., Washington, D.C. 20005.

to find the worthwhile materials. One way to shorten this process is to have in mind what one is looking for when one pages through the various journals that exist. The best way to "keep up" in education is to have one's own agenda and follow it out. If one tries to read the literature without a focus, one is quickly lost. One reason that a large number of teachers don't read the professional literature is that they have not discovered this elementary lesson.

What can one teacher do? He can work with the newly militant NEA to influence instructional decisions. He will find it receptive, even eager. The NEA has become an active agent at the local level in recent years—not only in the field of teacher welfare, but also in the field of instructional improvement.

Any teacher can work with his local NEA representatives toward including in the negotiated contract language that requires a majority of classroom teachers on local curriculum committees and that specifies that all matters of curriculum policy and practice be put under the control of such committees. The content of instruction, the evaluation schemes and instruments, the instructional materials, provision of time for in-service work—all of these can be made binding agreements, with the help of the revitalized NEA.

In entering this field of action, a teacher must accustom himself to the idea that the schools are political units, that the NEA is a political-professional organization, and that political action is required to move large-scale changes from talk to action. This is a new stance for teachers, though not for the better established professions, such as medicine, law, and accounting. Perhaps the teacher's first task is to confront himself as a political being.

What can one teacher do? He can decide what his own agenda will be—the one that fits his concerns and abilities best—and pursue it in his classroom, with his administrators, with his professional associations, in the colleges and universities, and in the professional literature.

The Administrators

There is one group of students of educational innovation who insist that significant innovation cannot come from within the system, but must come from outside the system and from the top down within it. From the outside in and top down. If this sounds harsh, it reflects a harsh judgment on the innovative quality of educational leaders. What can the administrator do?

Let's remember that innovation in education is finally carried out by the teachers in the classrooms and that they are fully capable of aborting the best laid plans if they don't understand or approve of them. One of the school systems in the country most noted for the large number of innovations it has undertaken is seriously fragmented because of a leadership failure repeated by a succession of superintendents. Without meaning to, they constructed a climate within the system that made it impossible for innovations to spread within the system. The Brownie points were for innovation, not imitation, and the result has been a highly competitive, noncooperative systemwide atmosphere.

The encouragement of innovation is a tricky business, as every administrator knows. We will make a few suggestions on the point here, but we make them humbly, realizing the complexity of the problem.

What teachers want from administrators is that the administrators express support of experimentation in the system. Many administrators give teachers the impression that they have little faith in the teachers' ability or disposition to experiment with anything. The problem is to decide how one's support of experimentation is to be expressed. Here are a few do's and don'ts:

• Don't ask for experimentation in a global, unspecified fashion. Don't exhort teachers to experiment and then return to your office. They won't, or at best, experimentation will be sporadic. It may very well be carried on by those teachers who are least secure and therefore most eager for the administrator's support. The best, most secure, and probably most imaginative teachers will be turned off.

• Offer specific support for experiments in being. Create a fund for experimentation within the school system, and allocate money from it in support of experiments when they emerge. Let everybody know that the fund exists and how they may have access to it.

• Make it clear that experimentation involves taking risks and that the administrator will support teachers who experiment even if mistakes are made. Nothing ventured, nothing gained.

• Create a curriculum council made up of administrators and teachers, meeting on school time, with substitutes provided to relieve teachers so that they may give the council their attention. Give this organization some power—which is to say some money. Let it identify areas in need of experimentation, and provide it with the time and funds necessary to carry out the experimentation that is called for. Supply it with consultants, but don't drown it with them. The consultants cannot do your thinking for you.

• Bend the rules for those who wish to experiment. Provide them with extra clerical help, if they need it, for a specified length of time. Don't ask that experiments necessarily be conducted within the existing framework. They often have to break the framework. One of the ways to discourage experimentation is to insist that the experiments be conducted within the existing school customs and habits. One experiment failed in a suburb of New York precisely because the principal insisted that in the name of evenhandedness the experimenting teachers do their work within the existing framework. He thought he was supporting the experiment. The teachers thought he was denying its meaning.

• Help the experimenting teachers with their public relations problem. The administrator is in a better position than anyone in the school system to awaken local awareness and interest. Teachers will interpret his work in this area as support of experimentation.

• Above all, tolerate mistakes. Teachers who experiment often are filled with zeal and will be carried away by their own enthusiasm. This tendency has to be recognized for what it is—a kind of overflow of excitement. The administrator can help by interpreting the excitement of the experimenting teacher to the teacher's peers and colleagues.

All of these do's and don'ts add up to support of experimentation. We repeat: the administrator who simply asks for experimentation without following through in this fashion cannot expect it to be carried on with any consistency.

The administrator is also a teacher. He, too, bears a responsibility toward his professional organizations. He, too, should be on the lookout for local programs in the colleges and universities. He, too, is an educational innovator.

* * * * * *

A final word on the source of ideas for innovation. We have tried to provide some ideas in the earlier pages of this book. We have not exhausted them, of course. One of the myths of education is that all the ideas have to come from within the school system. It doesn't matter where an idea comes from—outside or inside. What matters is how it is treated inside the system. We all want to be eclectic with respect to educational ideas. We suggest here that the ideas presented in these pages be used, but we claim no authority for them. The authority will develop in the school systems that make use of them, redeveloping them and making them fit local circumstances.

It can be done. We need not wait for permission from others to do it. We don't have to wait for federal funds to decide to individualize instruction and make a humane school. We don't even have to wait for public permission. If our interpretation of the times we live in is correct, we are facing not public apathy, but a public mandate to make a school such as we have never seen before—a school that has as its central purpose the building of legitimate grounds for self-respect.